Pip Williams was born in London, grew up in Sydney and now lives in the Adelaide Hills of South Australia with her family and an assortment of animals. She has spent most of her working life as a social researcher, studying what keeps us well and what helps us thrive. Her first novel, *The Dictionary of Lost Words*, based on her original research in the Oxford English Dictionary archives, was published in 2020 and became an international bestseller. This was followed by *The Bookbinder of Jericho*, a companion to *The Dictionary of Lost Words*, which again combined her talents for historical research and beautiful storytelling. *One Italian Summer* is a memoir of her family's travels in search of the good life, which was first published by Affirm Press in 2017 to wide acclaim.

PRAISE FOR *ONE ITALIAN SUMMER*

'*One Italian Summer* is delightfully witty and honest. You can feel the summer heat of Italy, not only in the scenes Pip describes, but in the wholeheartedly warm tone she speaks to us with. She conjures the warmth of Italy with great skill, and will leave you aching to go wandering through Italy. There is a deep love of place and life in this book, and above all, enduring love of family.'
Better Reading

'A book as rich and wise and full of goodness as the good life it seeks to define.'
Carol Lefevre, author of *Nights in the Asylum*

'A delightful, insightful book charting the adventures of one family whose quest for the good life in Italy brings with it the simple pleasures of the table and the hard graft of growing that food; Pip's elegant prose transported me deep into the heart of Tuscany and is the most eloquent advert for a working holiday I've ever read.'
Christine McCabe, author of *A Garden in the Hills*

'Warm as a Tuscan evening, generous as broken bread and honest enough to question whether happiness is really a hill of compost.'
Max Anderson, author of *Digger*

'They're dirty, they're tired, they're confused ... it's so real and she's such a good writer. It's a pleasure to read.'
Sarah Tooth on *The Book Club*, ABC Radio Adelaide

'A love story. A work story. A food story. A parenting story. A travel adventure story. The writing is elegant and deft, sensual and simple. As with all good memoirs, you will race through it then stare into the middle distance to ponder its subterranean truths and longings. You will think about your own life ... perhaps make plans of your own.'
Rebekah Clarkson, author of *Barking Dogs*

ONE ITALIAN SUMMER

affirm
press

First published by Affirm Press in 2017
This edition published in 2023
Boon Wurrung Country
28 Thistlethwaite Street,
South Melbourne, VIC 3205
affirmpress.com.au

10 9 8 7 6 5 4 3 2

 A catalogue record for this
book is available from the
National Library of Australia

ISBN: 9781922930477 (paperback)

Cover design by Emily Thiang
Typeset in Sabon by J&M Typesetting
Proudly printed in Australia by McPherson's Printing Group

This book is a work of non-fiction based on the author's experiences and memories.
All efforts have been made towards a truthful account. However, it is acknowledged
that others may recall events depicted in this book differently. While some dialogue is
verbatim, the majority reflects the meaning of conversations to the author, rather than
the actual words.

PIP WILLIAMS

ONE ITALIAN SUMMER

Across the world and back in search of the good life

affirm
press

For Shannon
For Aidan
For Riley
You make my life good

———

Bread.
It was my undoing.
And my salvation.
If it hadn't been for bread,
we might never have gone to Italy.

———

Rome

(Six impossible things before breakfast)

In a few hours Rome will be teeming with people, but now, at six in the morning, it's all ours. Woken by jetlag, we've emerged from our apartment on *Via Boccaccio* to search for breakfast, but we don't know which way to go. Shannon and the boys look perturbed, but my nerve endings still tingle from those first waking moments when Shannon's arm on my belly kept me from stirring. I lay listening in near darkness to the unfamiliar sounds of the street below: the rumble of a delivery van over cobblestone, the clatter of a security door, a shouted greeting and a conversation I could only guess the meaning of. I felt like a child eavesdropping on a secret.

It will take time for the city to wake, so we wander aimlessly, taking it in turns to hold one another's hands and squeezing lightly to assure ourselves we're really here. We favour the narrow lanes, and each turn reveals a treasure: domed churches, a covered archway with a frescoed ceiling, a wrought iron balcony. Then we see the hint of a private courtyard – the bough of an orange tree, heavy with ripe fruit, reaching out over a high stone wall. Aidan takes a running jump and tries to grab an orange, and I'm flung back ten years, to the front yard of our little house in Sydney.

'Front yard' might be an exaggeration; it was really just two square metres of dirt separating our front door from the footpath, but Shannon could see its potential. Like so many in the suburbs, we yearned for a slice of 'The Good Life', the kind of life where we could grow our own food and have a pet pig. Even before the boys were born, Shannon had begun dreaming of a honey-filled hive, a gaggle of geese and rows of lemon trees and apple trees and trees with fruit that nobody had ever heard of. As the house filled with toys and my days filled with mashed pumpkin and spilt milk, I'd begun to dream of baking my own bread and preserving home-grown pears.

But the dream was too big for our suburban box, so we lopped it and pruned it until all we could imagine was one small thing. That's when we planted a lemon tree in the front yard.

A couple of years passed. The boys grew bigger, the house grew smaller, our tree began to bear fruit. We were content.

And then our lemons started to go missing.

Allowing our lemon tree to overhang the footpath was a community service that we were more than happy to perform. If a neighbour sat down to grilled fish and realised they had no lemon, they could nip out their front door and pull one from our tree. No one should have to eat fish without lemon, and we had more than enough to share. But one evening I served up grilled salmon, and when we went to the tree, it was bare.

After a while, fruit returned. We talked of lemonade and lemon curd and lemon delicious pudding, and waited patiently for the fruit to ripen. When green gave way to yellow we stood on the doorstep of our little house, gazing like proud parents at what we had grown. But our pride and culinary optimism were short-lived. The next day, when we opened the front door, our tree was once again stripped of colour. There'd been enough lemons for everyone in the street to have fish that night, and suddenly they were all gone.

A door creaked open in the back of Shannon's mind and he began to walk towards it.

'Let's move,' he said.

'We can't afford to,' I said.

'We can if we leave Sydney.'

He was right. I liked the idea. We sold up and moved to the Adelaide Hills.

~

More than a thousand kilometres from Sydney, our dreams found expression in a two-bedroom stone cottage and five acres of farmland.

Shannon had a shed – a coming-of-age moment for any man who's found himself lingering in the hardware shop long after he's located the duct tape. He also had a canvas for all the ideas that had preoccupied him over the past few years, and a part-time job as a gardener that left him just enough time to implement some of them. He joined 'Trees for Life' and planted hundreds of native seedlings. He studied permaculture, built up beds for a vegetable garden and began planting fruit trees. Some I knew, others I'd never heard of. His eyes shone, and the skin on his cheeks flushed as if he were in the grip of a new love.

Our two boys, not yet at school, ranged free within their expanded borders. Aidan was finally able to kick a ball and swing a bat with no restrictions. He soon became adept at both – though the household budget now had a dedicated line for all the balls that kept getting lost in the long grass. He pulled carrots from the earth and ate them, soil and all. Riley didn't have the teeth for carrots, so he just ate the soil. I looked on, thrilled.

But I was still an observer. I hadn't so much down-shifted as side-shifted. I was barely able to get my hands dirty before I started to feel hampered by all the things I'd brought with me from Sydney. A job in the city paid the bills, and an unfinished degree demanded most of the attention I should have been paying to my pre-school children – and to our new pets, a pair of alpacas we'd bought in an effort to dress the boys in colourful home-spun woollens.

We entered into animal husbandry with exactly the kind of confidence you'd expect from well-educated city slickers with no idea. They were the first mammals I'd owned since killing my pet mouse, Millie, when I was eight (she overheated in the doll's clothes I dressed her in and died prematurely from eating too much chocolate), but at least Shannon had owned a dog, quite a large dog. Thanks to a few judicious suggestions from neighbours who were clearly concerned about animal welfare, we soon found that, leaving aside the spitting, alpacas are easier to care for than mice.

The alpacas gave up their fleece, and I found time to learn how to manage a spinning wheel – but in the way a nine-year-old with no particular talent manages the violin. I could move all the bits in the right way, but the final product could only be appreciated by those who loved me – and even they struggled. As for dressing my children in gorgeous hand-knitted garments, by the time I'd finished the first beanie, their heads had grown and they were old enough to insist they didn't want to 'look like Steiner kids'. I passed my misshapen masterpiece on to a friend with a child at the local Steiner school and bought the boys polyester footy beanies.

The spinning wheel soon found a home in the garage, along with the loom (what was I thinking?), the preserving kettle and about a hundred empty jam jars donated by friends. More and more artefacts of my dream started to pile up. Every time I tripped over something in my hurry to get in the car and off to work, I was reminded of how far from the idyll I actually was.

Then the life I sought finally found me. One glorious December I finished my degree and two work contracts, and my new job wouldn't start until February. Time, usually twisted and congested, became like an open road. There were hours, even days, to do nothing in particular, so I began making bread.

Since my early twenties, every two years or so I'd rolled up my sleeves and plunged my hands into a mound of flour in an earnest effort to make bread from scratch. The resulting brick, or sludge, would be nibbled politely by family and friends, but even their love didn't extend to a second bite, and eventually the loaf would be shot-put into the compost. Bread had become my nemesis. After each defeat I'd retreat, wounded, into the bread aisles of the local supermarkets.

It had been many years since I'd attempted to make bread, but I felt ready to try again. This time I enlisted the help of a good recipe book and I followed every step with meticulous care.

I brought forth bread.

Shannon and the boys ate the lot before the sun went down. I felt a warm stillness in my belly that could have been explained by the thick slice I'd devoured when it was hot from the oven, but which I knew was really pure, unadulterated happiness.

I began to bake regularly, always on a day when everyone was out of the house, when the silence and the hours asked nothing of me.

Those moments when the heel of my hand was stretching out an elastic dough, and I was panting a little from the effort of kneading, were some of my most euphoric. I'd feel like Nigella Lawson. 'You have to *dominate* the dough,' I'd say to the empty house in a posh English accent, and as soon as the dominating was over, I'd pop on the kettle. I'd always thought of bread making as time-consuming, but on those days time seemed more available than ever. Once kneaded, the bread required no more than my presence, and I was free to do nothing of any consequence to anyone, except me. I'd scribble a few lines in a beautiful notebook, bought soon after leaving Sydney but barely touched until I'd begun to bake. A few lines would turn to pages, I'd knock the dough back, make another pot of tea then read what I'd written. After a while the notebook was half-full, its pages dusted with flour, its cover crusty with dried dough. I felt like I'd planted something, and that with care it might grow.

Finally, our tree change was fulfilling all its promises. The chooks were laying, the fruit trees were fruiting and the alpacas had given up another fleece so I could make a few more lopsided beanies that no one would wear. Then summer ended and I started my new job. Time contracted and I felt out of breath (but not in a sexy Nigella way). I made bread on Thursdays. Then I made bread every second week. Then I stopped making bread.

For some people, a sign that things are out of control is skipping the gym or their daily meditation, or getting home from work after the kids have gone to bed. For me, it was Tip Top in the bread bin. 'Good on you, Mum,' rang caustically through my mind as I slapped cheese between two white slices and screamed at the kids, again, to hurry up because I was going to be late for work.

Our trees began to bend with the weight of fruit. Apples, plums, nectarines and Shannon's prized pluots ripened. But when the fruit started to fall we were too busy for bottling and we put it off, as if nature could be rescheduled. The apples turned floury before they dropped, but the stone fruit didn't let go until they were at their tastiest – all we caught were the pluots, the rest rotted and created a mess that we never had time to clean up. Shannon's cheeks lost their flush.

A dream kept safely locked away can be easily ignored. But when you release a dream you live with it, you go to sleep with it, you wake up with it, and you must negotiate with it on a daily basis. Our dream was holding us to account, and we felt the weight of its expectations every time we made a compromise.

I began seeing a psychologist for work-related stress. It seemed more acceptable to talk about work than bread. Could I seriously complain that a lack of baking was sending me into a dark hole? After six sessions I was still depressed, which is perhaps understandable when all we talked about were ways to 'reframe work priorities' and tackle insomnia – bread was never discussed. On the way home from the last session I stopped for a two-litre cask of red wine and a loaf of sliced white – it was my rock-bottom moment.

'Do you remember that fancy dress party we went to when we were first going out?' I was on my third post-counselling glass and we were watching *Survivor*.

Shannon struggled to put my question into context.

'All our friends came as movie stars and rock legends,' I reminded him, 'but you dressed as a hippy and I came as a rainforest.'

'I actually went as Neil from the *Young Ones*,' he said, 'and I vaguely remember being accused of not dressing up.'

'You chained yourself to my trunk and vowed to save me from the wheels of industry.'

'You're lucky I was there, I don't think the environment was a high priority for some of our friends.'

'We were both different in the same way.'

8

'Why are we talking about this?' Shannon asked.

I considered my next words. For years we'd been trying to live the good life, a slow and sustainable life, a life of meaningful production. That was our thing, what set us apart and brought us together. But so much of my time was spent in meetings where everything was 'moving forward', and my desire to move back seemed impossible. I was starting to feel endangered.

'I don't think we're living this life the way it should be lived,' I said.

'No, I don't think we are either,' Shannon agreed. 'It needs more time than we're giving it.'

That was the truth of it. Living simply couldn't be rushed. How could we grow food and preserve it, bake a good loaf and break it with friends, without going bonkers or broke?

'What if we made it pay?' suggested Shannon.

'How would we do that?'

'Grow more, make more, sell it at the farmers' market?'

Colour was rising in his cheeks, but draining from mine.

'It would need both of us, Shan. I'm already exhausted.'

'You could work less,' he said.

'I *could* work less.' A small flicker of something stirred in my chest. 'Or, better still, I could leave work altogether.' Saying it out loud was more therapeutic than the past three months of therapy. A cloud began to lift.

We looked around. We devoured television renditions of sustainable living: *River Cottage*, *Gourmet Farmer*, *Gardening Australia*. And when the remote control failed to find these top-shelf versions of our ideal life we'd settle for five minutes of *Backyard Blitz*, like a drunk taking a swig of turps. These programs made us want the good life more than ever, but they didn't really teach us anything about living it. Except for a vicarious sense of satisfaction, nothing about our daily existence really changed.

'We need real-life role models,' I said one night, after bingeing on Hugh Fearnley-Whittingstall's *River Cottage – Spring*. 'Hugh has an army of experts helping him out. We need to know how to do it ourselves.'

'So what do you suggest?' asked Shannon.

'Work experience, Shan. Some good, old-fashioned work experience.'

We decided to become WWOOFers – Willing Workers on Organic Farms. The deal was simple: we would work during the day getting hands-on experience, and in return we'd receive shelter, sustenance and cultural immersion.

We decided very quickly that Italy, home of the slow food movement, was the place to go. It had a similar climate to ours, pesto was Riley's favourite food and gelato was Aidan's. At the back of my mind there was also a memory of Rome from when I was eighteen and at the beginning of things. I'd been admired by a young man with light-brown eyes and dark-brown skin and a voice that felt like sun-warmed honey. He may have just been asking for directions to the Colosseum (who knows, my Italian was rubbish) but because it happened in that place and at that time it's lingered as one of those 'what if' moments.

It wasn't love I was seeking anymore, it was life, but Italy seemed the right place to go for a change of direction.

So we quit our jobs, took the boys out of school, left the house in the care of strangers, and flew to Rome.

~

I feel like Alice down the rabbit hole – fragments of life, past and present, flashing by as I fall. The lemons are all gone but these Roman oranges remain. They're too high, and Aidan's efforts to pick one are fruitless. The owners, I think, will have no need to flee their city life. I notice their heavy wooden door, the brass knocker shaped like a hand. I imagine knocking, being greeted by an old woman and led up a narrow staircase to an attic room – mine for as long as I want it – with a view of the city: a place to collect my thoughts and fill the notebook I bought before getting on the plane. Or perhaps I've knocked a hundred times before and the door will open on a familiar face, the one I met twenty-five years ago on that first visit to Rome, before Shannon, before Aidan, before Riley. His light-brown eyes will welcome me in …

'Muuum! Hurry up, we're hungry.'

We all have a 'before' and a thousand 'what ifs'. I catch up to the boys and take each by the hand, so grateful for what came after.

We've been walking for no more than fifteen minutes when we notice the sound of a steady rush of water. We emerge into a small but spectacular square – *Piazza di Trevi*. It's just after six, that time between night and day when dreams still dominate, and the impossible is easier to believe. Easter is approaching, and Rome is bursting with tourists and pilgrims. Every one of them will eventually make their way to this most famous of fountains. Some will throw in a coin, some will find a place to sit on the steps and write a postcard or, more likely, send a tweet – *Sitting on the steps of the Trevi Fountain. The crowds are insane.*

We stand alone, and in relative silence. It's our first morning in Rome and we have the Trevi Fountain all to ourselves.

Well, almost. A Roman wades in the freezing pool below Neptune and his sea horses. He's no Anita Ekberg (more like George Costanza) but he draws the eye. With broom in hand and nothing but a T-shirt and track pants to protect him from the bite of the cold morning, he sweeps the floor of the fountain to gather the treasure thrown in the previous day.

'People throw in a coin then make a wish,' I tell Riley.

'Can I?' he asks.

I give him some change and he walks to the edge of the pool.

Tears surprise me, slipping down my cheeks before I know they're there. I'm thinking about all the late nights on the internet looking for our beautiful apartment, all the emails to and from farms, the stress of finishing one last report, writing handover notes, wondering if that last research paper will ever get published and realising I no longer cared. Then the fiasco in the carpark a week before the end. I'd been tired for months, and in my daze I'd smashed into a bollard and mangled the side of the car. It woke me up, and I'm sure it saved my life – better a prang in an empty car park than on the freeway at a 110 kilometres per hour. It cleared away any doubts I had about whether we were doing the right thing, and I left the office on the last day like a hostage released.

Then I remember sitting on our bed, piles of clothes ready to be stuffed into backpacks. It was eight o'clock on a Friday night, and the house-sitters would arrive from New South Wales on Tuesday. On Wednesday we'd fly to Rome.

Riley's respiratory specialist called.

'I've been thinking about young Riley.'

'Oh, yes?' My armpits were prickling in the way armpits do when your subconscious has registered the seriousness of a situation, but your conscious mind is still blissfully unburdened.

'I don't think he should fly.'

'But we've had all the tests. You said he'd be fine.'

'There's a risk he'll suffer a spontaneous pneumothorax.'

'A what?'

'It's a collapsed lung, and the outcome could be dire.'

He really used that word. Suddenly my armpits and conscious mind were on the same page.

'But we leave in a few days.'

'Oh, is it that soon?'

'And we've organised house-sitters, they've rented out their house and put their furniture in storage. We have to go.'

I remembered Aidan jumping in the deep end of a pool before he could swim. I'd spent the first crucial seconds untying the laces of my left shoe before realising that my son's life was more valuable than a pair of sneakers. The specialist told me that if we put Riley on a plane bound for Europe, one of the many cysts that occupy what's left of his right lung might burst, his lung might collapse, and he might die.

'So what should we do?'

'Oh, that's up to you, really. It will probably be fine, but you just can't be sure.'

Or words to that effect.

What do you do with words to that effect? You have a panic attack. You hyperventilate. You say, 'Oh my God' over and over.

An hour later, after helping me regain control of my breathing with the aid of a paper bag, Shannon called the specialist back and insisted we have whatever tests were necessary to make an informed decision.

Twenty hours before our flight, I was staring at Riley's CT scans on a light box. The surgeon was explaining that most of his cysts were small, but there were a few considered medium and therefore more of a risk – though, in his opinion, a very small risk. Not big enough to change our plans. 'You shouldn't stop him from living a good life based on the unlikely chance that something might go wrong. He'd never do anything.'

After three days of holding my breath, I exhaled.

~

So here we are in Rome, without incident. Shannon has wrapped his arms around me in quiet acknowledgement of all that has led to this moment, Aidan is looking for a way to climb up to one of the marble horses and Riley is watching a portly Roman sweep up his wish from the bottom of Neptune's pool. I'm well on my way to believing six impossible things before breakfast.

What else can I say about Riley so that he might seem familiar? Like most kids, Riley is almost normal. It's true that he has a chronic lung condition that could, theoretically, cause all sorts of drama in his life, but so far it hasn't. And in an effort to keep up with his older brother, he's managed to get to the age of nine with the requisite number of skills.

Riley is sensitive and sometimes anxious, and considerable courage was needed for him to learn to ride a bike and swim across a pool. But in cricket he can knock the bails off with a throw from near the boundary, and in soccer he'll risk life and limb to stop the best team in under tens from scoring another goal. He can spell long words with tricky letter combinations, and when I've had another hard day at work, and I'm so tired and cranky that overcooking the pasta leads to an ugly rant, Riley has a way of calming me down with a well-timed hug and a reminder that it'll be okay because he likes his pasta mushy.

Right now, Riley has his back to me. His hands are deep in the pockets of his fleece, and he's still. Is he contemplating his life, like I am, or is he just counting all the euros and trying to work out how many chocolate-filled pastries they could buy? He's been awake for hours and still hasn't eaten breakfast.

Our sweeper fills his second bucket with coins and we wander off to continue our search for espresso and pastries. That's all we want, coffee and chocolate. But I'm forgetting where we are. This is wonderland. It's not until you look up from the map you've drawn for yourself that you realise you're not where you thought you would be.

A winged goddess has caught our eye. Riding high on her chariot she presides over the *Piazza Venezia*. As we move forward, we realise she has a twin. They are ostentatious flourishes on a white marble monolith known locally as the 'typewriter' but referred to in guide books as the 'National Monument to Victor Emanuel II'. Victor was the first king of a unified Italy. His monument is hideous, and if it was the only thing to see from *Piazza Venezia* we'd follow our plan and turn back the way we've come, but the boys have wandered towards a park.

They're leading us away from coffee, and Shannon's head is splitting, so I call out to come back. They don't come. Nor do they come at the second call or the third. I consider raising my voice and issuing a threat involving electronic games, but I don't feel like shouting. We follow in a lethargic way, intent on grabbing a hand each and pulling them in the direction of food. Then we see what they see. Shannon's head clears, I clap like an excited teenage girl, and all of a sudden no one is hungry.

Two thousand years of civilisation peels away from our view; in front are flagstones once trod by Julius Caesar. All that's left of the temple he dedicated to Venus Genetrix is three columns supporting an intricately carved marble top. Venus Genetrix is the goddess of motherhood and domesticity. In the circumstances, my decision not to shout at the boys is a good one.

Here we see the sun come up. Although it's been light, the city has hidden the sunrise. The first we see of it is an explosion of brightness through the archways of the Imperial Fora – a daily miracle that's been occurring for two thousand years and marks the first morning of our journey. I hug each child in turn and kiss Shannon on the mouth in a way that makes Aidan feign illness and Riley giggle.

I'm reluctant to leave the temple of Venus but the boys have lost interest, so we cross the road for a preview of the rest of the Roman Forum.

'I spy, with my little eye, something beginning with "C",' I say.

'Colosseum!' Riley shouts. Of course we go to it. We stroll up the wide street taking photos. The boys run ahead, then beckon us to hurry. The whole morning has been impossible, yet here we are, and it's good. Really good.

Commuters spilling from the nearby metro station are our cue to leave. We try to retrace our steps but get lost. The upside is that we find ourselves standing outside a bar, its warm interior glow seducing us to move in close.

'*Due caffè, due cioccolate e quattro pasticcini, per favore.*' Riley's been practising all morning.

We're foot-weary, but we still stand at the counter instead of sitting at one of the many empty tables. We learnt on our arrival yesterday that a cafe is called a bar, and an espresso that costs eighty cents if drunk standing may cost three euros to enjoy sitting down. Our savings have to last another four months, so we usher the children out of the seats they've sunk into and lean heavily against the counter.

The barista is having none of it. Perhaps it's Riley's earnest attempt to ask for a pastry in Italian. Maybe it's Aidan's voluble grumbling. I'd like to think it's the way I look him in the eye, beseeching him to be my rescuer, hinting that maybe we've met before, a long time ago. Whatever it is, he points towards a table.

'Sit, sit. Don't worry, sit.'

In my imagination, I reach across the bar, hold his head in my hands and kiss him full on the lips – his good looks make this easy, but even if he'd been a fleshy *signora* with a prickly moustache I'd have imagined the same.

I realise all of a sudden that I am smitten with Rome, with its baristas and fountain sweepers, with its coffee and pastries, with its layers and layers of history. Over the next week I develop a serious crush.

And then it's time to leave.

Tuscany

(Repose)

Stefan is waiting for us when we get off the train at Rassina. For some reason I'm surprised that he's here. Despite months of planning and a recent spate of emails, I'm still struggling to believe that complete strangers are willing to welcome a family of four from the other side of the world into their home.

With difficulty, Stefan opens the side door of a beaten-up white van. Hives and boxes, a ladder and various other bee keeper's tools take up most of the available space. We shove our packs into spaces they don't really fit, rubbing them against spent honey frames and intensifying the humid sweetness in the van. Then we sit, passive and shy, as Stefan manoeuvres through the town.

Rassina is somewhat disappointing. There's not enough weathered stone, no piazza fed by narrow cobbled lanes. Black bitumen leads us past concrete buildings and light industry – the shops are closed and some are fortified. It's Good Friday, but there's a sense that half these stores will never open. A nondescript bridge carries us over the river Arno, which limps between silted bends. It's not Rome, I have to admit, but I refuse to be disenchanted. When we overtake one of those tiny three-wheeled utilities, its tray filled with boxes of vegetables, I realise that this is where we stop being tourists and start being … what? Intrepid travellers? Volunteers? Farmers, perhaps? Or something else entirely? The possibilities send a tingle of excitement through my entire body, and I hug myself to keep it contained.

A few minutes out of town, concrete is beginning to give way to green fields watched over by houses built for function not form. Stefan asks about our journey. We tell him about the Colosseum, and the Trevi Fountain at dawn. When we run out of words a comfortable silence settles between us. We lean into a corner, leaving the main road behind. Aidan whispers in my ear that he's hungry.

'Will we be stopping for gelato soon?' he wants to know.

Aidan was quick to agree to four months off school, but he'd wanted some assurance that his cooperation on this family adventure would be rewarded. What, he asked, did Italy have to offer him that he couldn't get in the Adelaide Hills?

'Let's start with the Etruscans in 600BC …'

With misplaced excitement I began to tell him of Italy's rich history. I saw an opportunity to introduce him to Italian culture, its architecture, its food traditions. Thirty seconds into my three-hour seminar, Aidan stopped paying attention and started examining the contents of his right nostril.

Recognising another failed attempt to inspire my eldest son, I changed tack.

'Gelato,' I said.

His eyes locked onto mine, the booger's journey towards his open mouth momentarily suspended. I had his full attention and I hadn't even raised my voice or threatened to take his Nintendo DS away. I wanted more.

'Every day,' I continued.

He let the booger drop to the floor and beamed at me like I was the best mum in the world. I live for these moments. I took the opportunity to seal the deal, to trick my twelve-year-old homebody into leaving the sanctuary of his room – drawers full of Pokémon cards and precious Dungeons and Dragons paraphernalia – for the unknown pleasures and hardships of a working holiday in Italy. Making a mental note not to tread on the booger in my bare feet, I launched my final play.

'Twice a day! After lunch and dinner!' My voice had risen to an hysterical pitch, but Aidan was jumping up and down, clapping his hands and actually telling me, in real, audible words, that I was, indeed, the best mum in the whole wide world. He couldn't wait to go to Italy.

Gelato is his weakness and I exploited it, shamelessly. Within seconds he'd calculated the exact number of gelatos he would consume over the four-month period. He wanted to know if they would be one, two or three scoops, and whether we would have access to gelaterias when we were on farms. I began to calculate the cost of two gelatos a day times four people. When it reached four figures, I reached for a loophole.

'In the unlikely event we have to walk more than an hour to a gelateria, then you'll need to settle for some other treat.

But this is Italy we're talking about, they have gelato on every corner.'

When he isn't eating ice-cream, Aidan is imagining himself as a character in *Lord of the Rings*. On our first day in Italy, the ancient architecture of Rome furnished his imagination so vividly that his sword was perpetually unsheathed. Where we saw history, he saw one of the ancient cities of Middle Earth – orcs and goblins a constant threat. By day two, his imagination could no longer sustain him. Aidan needed something more tangible to justify the hours of wandering. Without it, he had every intention of spending the day with his books and DS, venturing to the bar downstairs only after lunch and dinner to order his favourite green apple gelato. I'd let out a frustrated breath, which Shannon recognised as a precursor to an argument.

'Did you know that somewhere in Rome you can buy Pokémon flavoured gelato?' Shannon said.

Within minutes of receiving this gem of information Aidan became our co-conspirator. The search was exhausting, if not exhaustive, but as we failed to find our holy grail, Pokémon gelato now hangs like a carrot in front of us, and we're committed to chasing it across the country.

~

The van climbs ever higher, and the road has become narrow and broken. Rassina is meant to be just a half-hour drive from the farm, but we've already been driving for forty-five minutes. The last gelateria was at the train station. When Stefan pulls off the road and the van stops in a roughly cleared patch of forest, my heart begins to race. His calm demeanour takes on a sinister edge, his suggestion that we should get out of the van seems suspicious. I look to Shannon, but he's oblivious. Standing with our backs to the shadows of the forest, I gather the boys in.

How could we have been so foolish? Getting into a stranger's van, putting our children in danger? Stefan gestures towards Shannon, an abrupt instruction to follow him to the back of the van. I try to protest – thinking of backpackers in the Australian outback – but Shannon is under a spell. The sweetness of honey, the warmth of the smile, the hypnotic drone of bees. Come into my parlour said the spider to the fly.

Imagine my delight (and mild shame), when Shannon emerges from behind the van looking like a stormtrooper from *Star Wars*. It only takes Aidan a second to join the men, and soon all three are heading off down the track to check the hives Stefan keeps in this part of the forest. When Aidan bounds back to me ten minutes later, his easy smile bodes well for our stay with this enigmatic bee keeper.

'… then he cut the branch off the tree and the bees just stayed on it, like a big ball of jelly, all wobbly and rippling. He knocked them into an empty hive, but they'll only stay if there's a queen, so he's going to put them in the van with us and take them home …'

Riley and I begin swatting at invisible bees. Aidan, who has thwarted all my attempts to teach him anything about Italy, has just absorbed something. What a relief. Now I can justify his long absence from school.

A symphony of drones becomes the soundtrack for the rest of our journey to the farm. I pull my gaze away from the hills and look towards the man driving.

Stefan has a similar build to Shannon: lean, the definition in his forearms suggesting a wiry strength. He and his wife, Ulrike, moved from Germany to Tuscany thirty years ago. They worked on a farm, and after a while decided that the lifestyle suited them. Twelve years ago they settled high in the Tuscan hills with their five children. They began keeping bees and hosting WWOOFers.

I'm now quite certain that Stefan means us no harm, but I'm still on first impressions: greying hair and sun-browned skin, a weathered face rendered beautiful by a frequent comfortable smile. He's attractive, and it occurs to me that Shannon might look similar in fifteen years. I turn back to the hills to hide my blush.

When we first started talking about this adventure I googled WWOOFing to see how other families had done it. I was hoping to get tips on travelling with kids and an insight into what to expect from the farms we worked on. There was very little, mostly travel blogs written by young men or women, but there was one written by an Australian family of four. Their favourite farm had been in Tuscany. Among descriptions of the stone house, the swimming pool, the work tending bees and baking cakes, there was the fact that the WWOOFing family had been comfortably housed in an apartment. It sounded more like a country retreat than a working farm. The perfect place to ease us into our WWOOFing life.

Now, we're nearly there. The forest closes around us as we negotiate the dirt track. I'm looking forward to settling into the apartment, putting our few things in place and making it home for three weeks. And I'm hoping we'll become friends with this family. Until now, I've never contemplated the alternative.

But the real anticipation is for what we'll do here and what we'll learn. I imagine a field of flowers, hives dotted around, the four of us collecting honey. Instead of wearing white overalls and a protective hood, I'm looking splendid in a sundress that I didn't actually bring because I could no longer fit into it. I can't sustain the fantasy and decide I'd rather be elbow-deep in curd, or perhaps kneading a sourdough loaf. I'm picturing an afternoon with Stefan showing us how to make the beeswax candles I saw in the back of the van, when the forest suddenly loosens its hold.

Wisteria-encrusted villas nestled into fertile slopes have furnished our preconceptions of the farms we would stay on. We tried to prepare ourselves for something more prosaic, but we knew we'd be disappointed if we travelled to the other side of the world and ended up with a magnificent view of a housing estate. When the van stops, we tumble out. There's no wisteria, but we see an old stone farmhouse and there's a collective sigh of relief. Clichés are inevitable when describing *Il Mulino* – it's a travel poster made real. The house dominates one side of the track we've come in on and a promising curl of smoke rises from its chimney, drawing the eye to the hills behind. The other side of the track, which disappears into the forest again, is occupied by a clutch of equally beautiful buildings. They look over the valley to an olive grove. Stefan tells us they include a studio and two apartments, and I couldn't be more pleased.

A girl of about thirteen – long blonde hair and the slight, androgynous frame of pre-adolescence – comes running up to the van, gesticulating towards a nearby cherry tree. A stream of German words reminds us of this family's heritage.

The source of her excitement is a swarm of bees, hanging like a giant gyrating fruit from an upper limb. Stefan removes the ladder from the back of the van, dons his stormtrooper headgear and begins the process of capturing the swarm.

Calm is needed around bees, and Stefan is its embodiment. With a smoking rag in one hand he scales the ladder to its highest rung. When it's clear he still can't reach the swarm, there's no frustrated shake of the head or German expletives. In one fluid movement he's perched on a higher branch. In another he's laid out along the limb supporting the bees.

Back on the ground, I'm fretting. He's not large, but neither is the limb. Marta, his daughter with the long blonde hair, keeps talking to him in a tone that reminds me of when the boys are telling me about their day at school while I get the dinner ready. I want her to be quiet, to let him concentrate. If I was up there on that limb with a swarm of bees, a few swift entreaties to 'hush' would be the limit of my conversation.

Dulled, eventually, by the smoke, the bees allow themselves to be knocked into a box. Stefan will rehouse them later, along with the bees that have travelled with us from the forest. Now, it's time for introductions. There is a beautiful young woman named Simona, Stefan and Ulrike's fourth child, and the toddler in her arms is her daughter, Amalie. Simona explains that her brothers, Giovanni and Herman, live on other parts of the farm, and that her sister Eva is studying in Florence.

Marta, so animated before, now hides behind her mother, her greeting muffled by the hand she holds constantly at her mouth. Mirroring her, Aidan and Riley fall in behind my skirt, mumbling something resembling 'hello' at each introduction.

Farm kids are essential to the success of this journey. As volunteers, Shannon and I will be working many hours a day. We want the boys to have friends and an opportunity to learn the language through play. Marta, who is a year older than Aidan, is the child we're pinning all our hopes on at this farm, but this level of shyness could mean three weeks of skirt dwelling.

With our offspring doing their best to avoid eye contact, Ulrike and I exchange one of those looks that transcend language and culture. In a practised move, we both bend our heads and whisper similar things in different tongues. All three children shift incrementally out of the shadows cast by their mothers. It's a start.

'Follow me,' Stefan says.

I have my fingers crossed for a view, but he turns us in the other direction and leads us up a goat track strung on each side with a makeshift washing line. We trot to keep up, passing the chicken yard and a small field dotted with hives and humming with bees (but devoid of flowers). When we get to the edge of the woods we stop. Stefan is holding open the door of a small log cabin, waiting for us to go in.

The 'woodhouse' hasn't been used since the previous summer, when Simona and Amalie had to vacate their apartment for paying guests. It's dark and dank and very cold. Stefan tells us that during the warmer months the apartments are a source of income the family can't afford to sacrifice. At this time of year there is usually one free, but at the moment they have relatives staying from Germany.

The whole space is about the size of a double bedroom. There's no kitchen, nowhere to sit, and the alcove that I initially assumed would contain a bathroom is piled from floor to ceiling with a mess of clothes and toys and boxes. It would be difficult living here with a baby, and this thought puts my initial disappointment into perspective. After all, it's not as if my children will be crawling around, eating the bugs that I've just noticed falling like snow from the damp ceiling – are they caterpillars? Yes, tiny caterpillars, all over the floor and the pot-belly stove and the two single beds.

Just two singles.

'Is there another bed?' I ask.

Seconds pass before Stefan replies. From his expression I think he may consider it an impertinent question. 'Maybe there is another mattress. I will look at Giovanni's house.'

Shannon stays in the woodhouse to help the boys make up their beds while I follow Stefan further up the goat track to the home of his eldest son. Giovanni lives in a yurt. It's round and ramshackle, and if I wasn't so desperate to find a double bed resting under its eave I might consider it a beautiful thing, nestled into the Tuscan hillside the way it is. Giovanni isn't home, so Stefan lets himself in and begins a thorough search.

Nothing. My lower lip begins to tremble.

The problem is that I don't know what's expected of us, or what I can reasonably ask for. And I can't decide if Stefan's calm response to everything is a sign of peace or callousness.

'Here.' Stefan has stopped to look under the yurt. On his hands and knees he begins to pull out a double mattress: slightly damp, but otherwise functional. My enthusiasm for this marvellous find must reveal more than I intended. Stefan returns my grin and punctuates it with a gentle reassuring laugh. 'You will sleep better now,' he says.

The mattress covers most of the free floor, but there's enough room to walk between the beds, and I'm satisfied no one will get trodden on during night excursions to the toilet. Stefan explains that the toilet and the shower are back down the goat track, past the house, past the apartments, around the corner, past the honey room and just at the top of the slope leading to the herb garden. Then he leaves us to unpack.

'It's quite an adventure isn't it, boys? Like camping, but way more comfortable.' They don't need convincing, and now I've said it out loud, neither do I. We're not tourists any more, we're farm hands. Shannon puts his arm around my shoulder and gives it a congratulatory squeeze.

~

Once we've sorted out how we'll sleep, shower and shit, we have to figure out how we'll eat. As volunteers we exchange our labour for all food and board. For this reason, and because of a complete lack of thought, we haven't brought any food with us. Not even an apple.

By one o'clock in the afternoon this seems remiss. Like orphans in a Dickens novel we hang around the steps leading to the kitchen door, hoping to detect signs of food. If Ulrike happens to throw scraps out of the window for the birds to fight over, I think Aidan and Riley will enter the fray without a second thought.

The boys' shyness is inherited. Neither Shannon nor I can summon the courage to walk up the steps and ask that our children be fed. We hover, we distract, we lie on our damp bed and read aloud from the *Roman Mysteries* by Caroline Lawrence, we follow the track into the forest and discover a river. We return to the steps below the kitchen and hover some more.

By two o'clock we can wait no longer, I climb the stairs to the main house and knock. Ulrike is standing at the sink washing a lettuce – promising. I ask if I can help, thinking that as an insider I'll gain more knowledge. She puts me to work cleaning and chopping carrots, and soon reveals that lunch will be ready at about 2.30.

We're ravenous when we sit down to eat, but it takes me a moment to respond to the offer of stew. There are twelve of us, sat snuggly around an ancient wooden table in the middle of a kitchen in a stone house in Tuscany, and we're about to have a long lunch. I pinch myself. It's real.

Shannon and I pile our plates with stewed vegetables, lettuce, and the most delicious homemade rye bread. Aidan resists. He's never embraced rye bread, doesn't eat lettuce and balks at stewed vegetables – he gets all three regardless, and I'm hoping he'll try it just to be polite. Riley has already consumed a slice of rye and is reaching for a second. I tell him to mop up the stew with his bread, but he wrinkles his nose. I let it go; the table is too crowded for a food fight.

We're given the afternoon to settle in and explore the farm, and at half past nine in the evening we gather in the kitchen to eat again. It's three hours past our usual dinnertime and two hours past the boys' bedtime, so we're less inclined to draw this meal out. We fill Riley up on more rye bread and manage to get Aidan to eat a few leaves of lettuce. When the plates are empty we wash up and say our goodnights to the family.

In single file we follow the path that takes us around the apartments and past the honey room. When we get to the top of the slope that leads to the herb garden, we stop. The bathroom is a shower, a sink and a Turkish toilet. The boys complain about squatting over a hole in the ground, so Shannon tells them to pee into the stinging nettles that surround the doorway. A joke hangs in the air, but we're all too exhausted to claim it.

I'm the only one who straddles the porcelain hole, and I regret not having stronger thighs. By the time I straighten up, the energy required for a shower is beyond me. We stumble up the goat track in silence and fall into our beds.

Riley falls asleep almost immediately but Aidan is still hungry, so Shannon digs around in his pack for the chocolate eggs we've been saving for Easter Sunday. He lets him eat three. Aidan is easily pleased by chocolaty treats and his humour is instantly restored. With relief, we blow kisses towards his smiling face and watch his eyes close on this unusual day. Then we snuggle down to debrief in whispers.

'Mood enhancer,' Shannon says, passing me a chocolate egg.

'What are you suggesting?' I say.

'Well, it's been a big day, a strange day, and I noticed there was no wine on the table at dinner.'

'Yeah, I noticed that too. But you'll be pleased to know that I didn't need it.'

'You've never *needed* it.'

'I didn't want to worry you, but if I hadn't been able to fill one of those huge glasses with shiraz at the end of the day I might have started playing the pokies or googling cat videos or watching *I'm a Celebrity, Get Me Out of Here*. I *needed* something to quiet my mind.'

'Reality TV? I didn't realise how serious it was.'

'It shouldn't have been,' I say, a little ashamed. 'Nothing about my work is particularly important in the grand scheme of things.'

'*Was* important – it's not what you do anymore.'

I laugh. 'It doesn't seem quite real. But now I think about it, there's something liberating about spending the day with nothing to worry about except food and shelter and fitting in. That stuff really does matter.'

'And look at us – fed and sheltered and on the way to fitting in'.

'No red wine sedative required.'

'Here's to that.' Shannon raises his chocolate egg in the air and I raise mine. We tap them together then pop them in our mouths.

~

We wake on the first morning to a biting cold that we didn't expect of an Italian spring. The mountains are keen to hang on to winter for a little longer, and we're forced to wear most of our clothes to stay warm. Aidan wants to stay in bed. We can't convince him otherwise so decide not to push it. Riley offers Shannon and me a hand each, and we swing him down the path towards the house.

Ulrike has prepared a large pot of porridge for breakfast. Honey is a feature of most meals at *Il Mulino*, but it is best suited to breakfast. Riley, who must be a distant relative of Winnie-the-Pooh, spoons huge amounts into his bowl, and ours. It magnifies the oats, turning them sepia.

People come in and out of the kitchen. They fill bowls, slice bread. Some sit, others take their breakfast with them. Shannon and I pat ourselves on the back for adjusting to our new circumstances and marvel at how accepting the boys are – the rebellion we've been waiting for might not come. When Stefan sits down at the table, the porridge pot is empty, so he takes a thick slice of bread. I wonder briefly what Aidan will have for breakfast and make a mental note to ask about eggs.

Stefan tells us about the schedule of work. Actually, 'schedule' is too rigid a word. Life at *Il Mulino* is much more organic, and activity is dictated by need: if the grass is long it will be cut, if the walnuts are falling they'll be gathered, if there are weeds they'll be pulled. It's as if the industrial revolution never happened. The only activities that have a regular rhythm are associated with eating, Amalie or the bees – and we don't need an alarm to be reminded of those.

'What are you smiling about?' Shannon asks.

'Alarm clocks. I've always hated ours, but I've never realised how perfect that name is.'

'How so?'

'It alarms me,' I say, spooning porridge into my mouth and recalling the small panic I would wake with, then the lingering fear. 'Remind me to get rid of it when we get home,' I add.

On our first day I get to know Amalie and all her lovely little ways, while Shannon accompanies Stefan to check on hives.

Babysitting isn't quite what I had in mind when I committed to volunteering on organic farms, but it's the perfect activity to ease our family into a WWOOFing way of life. I can include the boys in whatever I'm doing with Amalie, and they make babysitting a whole lot easier than it might otherwise be. Riley gets more pleasure out of playing with squeaky balls than I do, and when I tire of reading *Dieci Coniglietti* (Ten Little Bunnies) the boys can take over. It's win, win, win – Simona gets to earn some money attending to the needs of an old woman in a nearby village, Ulrike can get on with baking and washing and tending her greenhouse, and the boys and I learn how to count to ten in Italian.

With Amalie on my hip I have an excuse to wander into the kitchen whenever I like. The loaf left on the kitchen table tempts us, and Riley and I snack on slices of rye all morning. Aidan snacks on nothing. At lunchtime he leaves a plate of brown rice and vegetables untouched, and drinks three glasses of apple juice. He's tired, he says, so I suggest an afternoon nap.

Once I've handed Amalie over to her work-weary mother, I begin weeding around the lettuces in the greenhouse. Marta and Riley have been playing table tennis nearby for the best part of an hour, and every few minutes I hear Marta's stilted English declaring the score. She is winning, but not by as much as she could be, and when I hear them laugh I'm grateful that this quiet girl is willing to share her home and her time with my quiet boy.

The product of my afternoon's labour is two buckets of weeds. I empty them on a compost pile then take the track up to the woodhouse to check on Aidan. He's been resting a long time, and I suspect some sneaky DS play. I compose my lecture: it's light on reproach and heavy on enticement – table tennis should draw him out without fuss.

Aidan isn't on the DS. He's lying on his side and staring at the wall. I walk around our mattress and sit on the edge of his. Vomit has stuck to his chin.

'Aidan, what's wrong?'

'I don't feel well.'

I get him up and hand him a drink bottle, but he needs to be sick again. We hurry out the door and he retches into the scrub beside the cabin. The stuff is liquid, slightly yellow – not a scrap of half-digested food. Not quite the protest I was anticipating. I have no way of reasoning with this.

I realise that Aidan hasn't eaten properly for two days and has filled his belly with water, apple juice and a tiny bit of chocolate.

We've been so preoccupied with being good wwoofers that we barely noticed. His pale face and bile are my reproof – I never did remember to ask about eggs for his breakfast.

I put my arm around his shoulders and lead him down the path to the kitchen. I don't know what I'll feed him, but feed him I will. In the end it's Ulrike who comes to the rescue. She's just made an apple cake. Aidan eats two slices then bounds out of the kitchen, all smiles, to find Riley and Marta. This is his superpower; the physical and emotional insults of life just don't stick to him. It's not a trait he inherited from me.

I slide into a chair and let Ulrike cut me a thick wedge.

'Sometimes Marta refuses to eat my bread, so when I go into the village I usually buy some white rolls,' Ulrike says, walking over to a large wooden chest. She lifts the lid on her emergency stash. 'Please, give to Aidan when you want.'

I feel less like a stranger.

~

The next day is Easter Sunday. No work, just feasting and a walk.

The family mostly eat vegetarian, but Ulrike has swapped some honey and potatoes for a goat from a nearby farm. It's to be the centrepiece of an Easter feast that includes cake for breakfast and a chocolate egg hunt for the children. The tortellini with sage butter and crostini with pesto are a hit with Aidan and Riley, who eat more at this meal than in the entire first two days on the farm. But the goat is what we're all waiting for. Having seen it enter the kitchen, head and little white tufted tail attached, we're curious about how it will end up on our plates.

It comes out in pieces, nothing fancy. It's not a 'dish' – deconstructed, reconstructed, 'pulled' or served with a suspicious looking 'smear' for presentation on social media. It's food, real food, to be shared in real time. For this family, eating meat is a celebration, and we spend a surprising amount of time talking about the goat – its origins, its age, what it was fed. I think of how casually I'd throw a vacuum-sealed cut of meat into my shopping trolley back home, crossing my fingers it wasn't fed with hormones, but in too much of a hurry to bother with the fine print.

'Would you like to see where the goat came from?' Stefan asks me.

'Yes, we'd love too. Is it far?'

'Not so far.' He puts Amalie on his back and leads the way to a forest track.

Not far, he said. Two hours later, after much huffing, puffing and a fair bit of stopping 'to look at the view' (even when there was no view to look at), we arrive at a farm perched on the top of a ridge.

'There is the daddy,' says Stefan, pointing to a huge goat clearly intent on connecting its horns with anyone fool enough to come close to its enclosure.

'Don't tell him we just ate his kid,' says Aidan. But it doesn't translate, and only we laugh.

The farm is beautiful: only a few acres of land, with vegetables and goats and an old horse. Like Stefan and Ulrike, the owners probably have access to the chestnuts that grow throughout the forest, and I'd bet my life there's an olive grove on the other side of the ridge.

'We could do this,' I whisper to Shannon.

'I reckon we could,' he whispers back.

'And if we get goats, we could have our own milk as well as meat, and I could make goat's cheese.'

He exaggerates a sour face.

'You'd get used to it,' I say.

'If you can get used to waking at dawn to do the milking, I promise I'll get used to goat's milk.'

How will I do that without an alarm clock? I think.

The walk home is mostly downhill, and I have breath for conversation. This whole region is dotted with villages perched precariously on hillsides, all stone and slate and terracotta. I can imagine renting one of the stone houses – just me, a notebook and a pile of novels – having amusing misunderstandings with my neighbours and flirting with the young mechanic who fixes my moped after I break down in the narrow lane behind the olive grove. But the reality, according to Stefan, is rather less romantic. Many of these villages are being abandoned due to a lack of work and a move away from subsistence farming. As more and more families leave, the local schools are closing and only a few villages still have a post office and store.

'They don't look abandoned,' I say.

'No, city people buy the old houses and renovate them, but they don't have time to stay in them, so usually they are empty.'

My moped mechanic disappears, and I realise I have imagined, more or less, the storyline of *Under the Tuscan Sun*.

Not very original, Shannon will say, when I share it with him later.

~

It's almost time for lunch on our seventh day at *Il Mulino*, and Amalie and I are both waiting, desperate to see Simona's little car emerge from the woods. Until it does, Amalie is willing to cling to me, legs draped around my right hip, her head in the hollow below my collarbone. She's a bird child, and I'm a temporary nest.

Over the past week we've discovered just how much work the good life can be. As well as helping Stefan with the hives, Shannon has been spending his time reclaiming the overgrown herb garden and cutting back grass in hard-to-reach places. Back home, grass is the bane of Shannon's life – unfortunately, it just keeps growing. Stefan has a similar relationship with it, and he displayed uncharacteristic enthusiasm for Shannon's experience with a brush-cutter. Cutting grass has become Shannon's thing.

My thing, in the mornings at least, has been looking after Amalie and helping Ulrike in the kitchen. Aidan and Riley lost interest in Amalie after a couple of days, so babysitting has become more of a chore. The boys would prefer to be down at the river skimming stones than reading *Dieci Coniglietti*. Amalie insists on it, and I've begun counting rabbits in my sleep.

We hear the engine at the same time. Amalie raises her head from my chest and points towards the car. When it comes to a stop I put her down so she can toddle towards her mother. Twin smiles, like magnets, pull them closer together.

In the afternoon Ulrike and I sit side by side amongst the raspberry canes. We're like passengers on a train, gossiping to pass the time as we make the slow journey from one end of a row to the other, pruning some canes and tying others. We sit in the dirt, two metres apart. When I shuffle along, the odd thistle spikes me, and when I reach with secateurs to snip new growth I'm stung by the nettles lying in wait. I'm getting used to the nettles, though I'm not immune like Ulrike. She can grab great bunches with bare hands; I've insisted on gloves. Yesterday she had me collect a bag-full. Some went in our dinner, while the rest is drying and will be used for tea.

Ulrike is telling me about other WWOOFers, about a couple who were meant to stay for two weeks but disappeared after a few days when paying guests arrived and the pair were asked to move from the apartment to a small room above the toolshed.

'They did not work too hard; they had a car and spent much time visiting other towns. The day after they moved from the apartment they went for sight-seeing in the afternoon and never came back,' Ulrike smiles and tilts her head in a bemused way. 'We were worried, of course, but when we checked their room it was empty – they had packed up in secret.'

'I hope they're the exception,' I say.

'Some WWOOFers just come for a holiday, they don't want to do real work. Others want to experience something different – it doesn't matter what. They often don't know very much, and at first they are a lot of work because they don't know what is a weed and what is a tomato. But they all learn eventually, and if they stay a while it is good for us all.'

We're neither of these, I think, pausing in my pruning while I wait for Ulrike to continue.

'It is unusual to have wwoofers who live on a farm,' she says.

I thought we might be in a category of our own. I lean forward and snip several canes, one after the other, just a little pleased with my efficiency.

'Stefan is so happy to have Shannon here,' Ulrike says. 'He knows how to use the equipment and does not have to be watched. Even with the bees he is learning fast. Already Stefan talks with sadness about him leaving. He is making Stefan's days easier.'

I nod, agree that Shannon is wonderful and wait for her to go on, but she doesn't. She has nothing else to say. Or perhaps she's just thinking how to say it. Trying to translate her praise for my skills from German into English without it coming out too soppy. I keep up my rhythm, increase my pace, *snip*, *snip*, *snip*, barely a twinge when the nettle gets me. Then she stops her pruning and turns to look at me.

I'm nodding, though she hasn't actually said anything yet.

'The way you are cutting the canes,' she says.

'Yes,' I keep nodding.

'I have just noticed, you have been cutting the wrong parts.'

'What? But I thought …'

'It is a common mistake the first time. It won't matter much, we always have too many raspberries.'

Ulrike stays with me until she's certain I know what to snip and what to save, then she leaves to get dinner ready and I travel the last hour alone. I reach the end of the row as the light is fading. My back is aching and the scratches on my arms from the fine raspberry hairs are beginning to swell and itch, but behind me is a long row of raspberry canes, neatly tied, with a barely noticeable patch of over-pruning. Despite a fleeting loss of face, I feel I've accomplished something worthwhile. When I drag myself across the threshold of the woodhouse it's almost eight. Dinner is probably an hour away, so I grab our toiletry bag and a towel and head back down the track to the shower.

Careful not to step into the toilet, I close the door and hang my towel on the hook above the window. Just thinking of hot water falling down my back unties a knot or two, and it occurs to me that I rarely feel the ache of a good day's work, or the satisfaction. Which isn't to say I'm free of aches and pains. I could sponsor a small village with all the money I've spent at the chiropractor trying to release my neck and shoulders from the pain of sitting in front of a computer all day. For the past few years I've rarely been without the tensions of my job, and when they stop me from sleeping or cause me to move like C3PO, there is nothing satisfying about the sensation. The ache I have now feels more like I've climbed a mountain. It's exhilarating, and my body, I decide, will get used to the labour.

Naked, I step into the shower, both hands cupped like a beggar's, reaching for the warm water.

'Shit! It's freezing!'

Five minutes later, the water is still freezing. I put my dirty clothes back on and drag myself up the track to the woodhouse. I ignore the boys, still playing on their DSs three hours after they should have stopped, and fling myself onto the bed. I feel less like a mountaineer with every passing minute, but then a moment of clarity shames me – Shannon is still out there, despite the fading light, cutting grass or chopping wood. He's been at it for ten hours. That's the downside of spurning the clock and following nature's cues – the lengthening days of spring and summer encourage farmers to work longer. Shannon will come back, stinking and tired, and when he finds out there's no hot water he'll shrug it off without complaint.

I'll put on some deodorant and pretend it didn't bother me either.

~

Stalls are already up for Arezzo's monthly market, their owners arranging produce or wares. Stefan helps arrange the trestle table and the small marquee, then leaves to check hives in a forest somewhere. He has over one hundred hives, scattered over as many kilometres, and much of his time is spent checking them. He's particularly vigilant after having lost most of his bees two years ago to a nasty little mite aptly named *Varro destructor*. It devastated their business and they nearly gave up this life they're sharing with us now.

'I will be back at midday to help pack up,' he says.

We have four hours. Ulrike's stall is near one end of the longest market I've ever seen. The centre of Arezzo is at the other. Jars of honey are lifted from boxes and placed in rows on the table, gradations of gold depending on when it was collected and what trees were in blossom. Acacia honey fetches the most money, and it glints in the sun as if it knows its worth.

We walk the length of the market – two kilometres – without stopping once to taste cheese or marvel at the varieties of pasta. When Stefan suggested we come to Arezzo he spoke of the market, full of the flavours and colours of Italy, and the medieval town centre. We agreed enthusiastically, but coffee, not sightseeing, was the real reason for our excitement. We had grown accustomed to an early morning, mid-morning and afternoon *caffè* while living in our Roman apartment, but coffee is not part of life at *Il Mulino*. Stefan and Ulrike don't drink it and Shannon, quite the addict, suffered terrible headaches for the first few days of our stay. Arezzo means cafes, and cafes mean real coffee, well made. We practically run those two kilometres.

Three women in matching pink aprons are crowded behind the counter of the first *alimentari* we come to. Their arms are elastic as they reach up and down and around to fill baskets and bags with loaves, cheese, olives. We wait – this prelude to coffee like delicate foreplay. When it's our turn, we order two *caffè* and two flat, white rolls filled with mortadella and provolone cheese. Our pleasure is quick, and we're back on the street before the boys have taken two bites of their breakfast.

Now we can concentrate on Arezzo. We head to *Piazza Grande* and sit on the steps of the old Tribunal Palace to consult our guidebook.

'On the first weekend of every month a huge antiques fair takes over *Piazza Grande*.' Shannon reads. Our timing is perfect.

The sloping piazza is protected on all sides by a collection of aged buildings that stand like books crowded on warped shelves. Stall holders are arranging their wares, adjusting their awnings. A few people browse, but it's still early. The piazza is just the beginning: the stalls spill down streets and lanes. There are wardrobes and chairs, old doors and sideboards, boxes full of treasure and trash.

We weave the boys past curiosities large and small. Five euros each to spend on whatever they like. They choose Pokémon cards, found in a box with some old comics. The words are Italian, but Aidan and Riley know the characters and find they can translate the text. Beyond the antiques we wander past a palace and along the ancient city wall. The boys begin to complain about too much lingering, but a large slice of potato and rosemary pizza has them following us in silence. We take a chance and enter the *Basilica di San Francesco*.

There's something so moving about a church filled with 700-year-old frescos. It isn't the subject that stirs me – representations of Mary, eyes downcast, not a single line on her brow to indicate she was up half the night with a colicky Jesus. Or the other Mary, on her knees and cleaning the feet of a man old enough to do it for himself while other men look on. What my eyes devour are the colours and lines that spread across the fractured stucco, barely illuminated by the sixty-watt bulb hanging from the vaulted ceiling. I probably shouldn't, but I can't help tracing a finger over the fading colour and imagining what life was like for the people of Arezzo in 1455, when Piero della Francesca painted these frescos.

Retracing our steps, we explore the weekly market at a leisurely pace. We walk past produce stalls crowded with rounds of cheese, the sellers passing us slices to taste on long, slender knives. My poor Italian cripples my intent to buy: there's so much choice but I can't read the descriptions, and since few of the sellers speak English, asking what kind of cheese this is, or how hot the salami might be is pointless – I can't make sense of the response and wind up staring back dumbstruck. I learnt in Rome that *dolce* means sweet and is used to describe a mild cheese. I say '*Dolce*?' and the ruddy-cheeked man with the knife grabs a round of cheese and cuts me a wedge. We'll eat it with mortadella, which I thankfully recognise, and crusty white bread when our stomachs can no longer wait for the call to lunch.

Then I see something else I recognise. I point and hand over five euros. In return I receive what looks like a charred ball of dung. It demands to be sniffed, so I rub my nose against its rough surface. I'm a slave to some smells – ground coffee closes my eyes in pleasure, jasmine draws out a smile for the approaching summer, coal smoke conjures an English infancy I can't recall and pizza is a mouth-watering promise that has only ever been delivered in Italy. Truffle has one of those top-shelf smells, too expensive to satisfy. In the Adelaide Central Market it can be found at the Mushroom Man's stall, behind glass in a straw-lined box. I sometimes sit at Lucia's, the Italian cafe opposite, and imagine I can afford to buy it. But I can't so I settle for truffle oil – which, as I've recently found out, usually doesn't contain any truffle at all.

Eyes closed, short frequent breaths, a low moan: I must look like I'm having an orgasm. Shannon recognises it and suggests I give up my prize – he actually tries to take it from me. No words, just an odd tussle as I try to bring the truffle closer to my nose and Shannon tries to extract it, while at the same time shielding our children from their mother's fetish. Shannon wins. He puts the truffle in his daypack, and in a moment my head is clear and my eyes have refocused. I start to think of what I will do with my ugly lump of fungus, and we walk on.

Ducks and chickens, alive and dead, give way to T-shirts made in China, with English slogans that will be meaningless to those who'll wear them. I'm surprised to see whitegoods and curtains, and realise that this market is the equivalent of a department store. Everything is here and everyone comes.

Back at Ulrike's stall, she smiles and asks if we liked what we saw. I tell her about the frescos and she nods; she knows how good they are.

~

I never thought we'd get used to the woodhouse, but we have. Everything we own has a nook or cranny, and it's become familiar, even comfortable. I'm a little bit proud. The only thing that has eluded us is hygiene – we stink.

It's been more than a week since we last bathed. The long trek to the bathroom has failed, repeatedly, to result in a hot shower. Only today I found out why: water at *Il Mulino* is heated by a wood fire, sporadically lit. With no idea of when the boiler got fired up we've somehow managed to time our showers with the off-days, when the water has cooled to just above freezing.

But we haven't been completely feral. We made ourselves an ensuite bathroom from a tap that leaks mountain water onto a mossy stone just beside the woodhouse. Ferns and grasses lend it the exotic character of an air-freshener advert – *mountain pine*, it would be called. It means we've had somewhere to brush our teeth and wash our hands after we've hidden in the undergrowth for a wee. The woodhouse is surrounded by undergrowth. It's a tangle of noxious weeds and ferns that have escaped Stefan's brush-cutter and become a breeding ground for ticks. I only know this because a tick the size of my fingernail burrowed its head so far into my thigh during a recent squat that not even Ulrike's expert hand could dislodge it. She assured me it was not the paralysis kind, but I immediately shifted all ablutions to the Turkish toilet on the other side of the farm.

My first hot shower since arriving at *Il Mulino* is such a profound pleasure that I'm actually glad for all the days of deprivation. Hot water travels down the length of my spine like the fingers of a masseuse, expertly working away at every point of tension. A long exhalation and I throw my head back to soak my hair.

'I hope you left some hot water for the rest of us,' Shannon says when I step out and he steps in.

'It doesn't matter if you didn't,' says Aidan, 'I don't mind missing out.'

Their drenching is short but effective. We leave the bathroom in a fog and glide towards the goat track. I feel reborn. My thinking is clearer, my body stronger, I must be more beautiful. I'm trying to think of a way Shannon and I can keep the boys out of the woodhouse for an hour or so when Stefan stops us.

'You can move this afternoon,' he says.

At first I think we're being asked to leave, that we've used too much hot water and violated the conditions of our stay. But as my post-shower euphoria wanes, Stefan smiles his gentle smile and continues.

'You can move into the apartment.'

It takes a second to realise that my recent affection for the woodhouse was just a story I told myself. I want to drop to my knees and kiss Stefan's feet, but instead I let out an indiscreet *whoop* and turn to high-five the boys. They seem less excited, perhaps even put out. Maybe they really are comfortable in the woodhouse or – an unsettling thought – maybe they don't like change.

The apartment has a sit-down toilet and functional shower, and it's quintessentially Tuscan. It occupies the ground floor of a restored stone house, and the shuttered windows open on a view of terraced gardens and olive groves. The picture inside is equally authentic, with whitewashed walls, tiled floors and a print of Michelangelo's *Genesis* above our double bed – the one where God is reaching his hand towards Man, who seems just out of reach and, in my opinion, a bit reluctant. For Shannon and me, the thick stone wall and wooden door separating our bedroom from the lounge room (and the boys' fold-out double bed) is a secret cause for celebration, but out loud, Shannon nominates the stove and little coffee pot as his favourite improvement. The boys vote for the fridge and its capacity to store cheese and mortadella, and I claim the reading lamp and armchair, where I'm determined to transcribe our days in comfort.

We're soon in a comfortable routine that reminds us a little of home. We still work about ten hours a day, but now those hours seem a doddle. It's easy to imagine staying for the whole summer.

~

Amalie is strapped to my back and we're negotiating the steep path down to the herb garden. Shannon is intent on revealing long-buried paths around the beds, spreading them with mulch to retard the growth of weeds. I recognise the industry of his movements, each action bringing him closer to a satisfactory outcome. For years now, I've longed for this. So much of my work as a social scientist has been spent on infertile soil: months developing a research grant that gets rejected. Not always because it wasn't good enough, but because there were so many others applying for money from such a small purse. The last grant and the one before that probably weren't good enough. I'm no different to Skinner's rats – without reward my enthusiasm began to wane. I started out with a noble motivation to contribute to the greater good, but found myself, twenty years later, concerned more about the money and less about the cause. And then there was that seminar.

I was presenting the findings of a four-year study of people's experiences living on the outskirts of four Australian cities – no jobs, poor public transport, nothing for teenagers to do, isolated mothers blah, blah, blah.

'Your findings are exactly the same as those from a few studies conducted in the 1960s and '70s,' said a slouching sociologist who looked like he'd been there at the time.

'And why do you think that might be?' I responded, a little nervous because I should have known more about those studies but had never made the time to read them properly.

'I think it might be because boxes on hillsides are easy money and infrastructure eats into the profits. It's good research, but it didn't make a difference forty years ago, so it probably won't make a difference now.'

'Well, I'd better pack up and go home then,' I said. He clearly thought that would be absurd. If every academic lived by that rule our tertiary institutions would be half empty.

It took me a while, but I finally did pack up and go home. And now I've decided I want to do work that's meaningful and enjoyable, that treads lightly and responds to natural cycles and real need. I want to get dirt under my fingernails, plant things and nurture them, then pull them out of the ground and feed them to my kids. This would satisfy me. This would be rewarding toil. But I'm a child of the clock. There's a lot to undo, and a lot to learn.

Shannon crouches, puts a finger in his mouth and blows up his cheeks. *Pop!* Amalie giggles and reaches her arm towards him. I obey.

'Mulch, Amalie, is the key to any efficient garden. Without it, you'll need to do so much weeding and watering there'll never be time for all the important things in life, like ...' His finger reaches again into the recess of his cheek, Amalie raises her own. Shannon *pops*, Amalie slides her finger in and out, unperturbed by the silence of the action. I'm not sure who is more delighted. Probably me.

The boys are sitting on the grassy slope, their school books open for the first time since leaving Australia. We've struck a deal. If they complete one page of maths and one of English, they can spend an hour on their DSs. We'll check their work when we stop for lunch.

'Dad, what's an acute angle?' Riley is looking down the slope. The old limbs of a chestnut reach over his head, stone buildings shadow his back. Shannon pulls an un-popped finger from his cheek, but I get in first.

'It's smaller than a right angle. Think of it as small and cute.'

The boys have learned not to ask me maths questions because I can rarely help without looking something up. In that frantic time between getting home from work and putting the boys to bed, looking something up was an inconvenience.

Riley looks to his dad for confirmation and receives a nod. He returns to his workbook. Shannon returns to his mulch. I sit on a rock at the edge of the garden and let Amalie play with my hair.

This is a moment. One I want to preserve for its balance and grace. Each of us doing something small but meaningful in the same space, not bothered by the passing of time. We've shed our outer garments and they litter the bank that is the boys' classroom. Spring is asserting itself and I feel myself relaxing into this life.

~

Simona is in the apartment upstairs, resting. Amalie is finally asleep. The soundtrack of the film that inspired her name leaks through the floor into our apartment. We've shared lunch and Ulrike is having her 'repose'. This is the word she always uses as she rises from the table after lunch.

'I am going for repose,' she says.

Each time, I'm tempted to translate and make her aware of the more commonly used 'rest' or 'lie-down'. Repose, though, is perfect. Ulrike is seeking quiet solitude. From the moment she wakes until the moment she goes to bed, she's occupied with the labours of the farm, her children, her grandchild, WWOOFers. A tranquil hour in the middle of it all is the pivot on which her day rests. It sustains the calm dignity that moves her from one task to another. I've already started to imitate her slow pace, though with enormous difficulty. Where I come from, there aren't many external rewards for going slow. I decide that from now on, I'll divide my days with repose.

But I'll have to start tomorrow – today there is school work to check. Shannon is exploring fractions with Riley and I'm trying to explain to Aidan why apostrophes matter. The time for repose passes, and Ulrike, refreshed, calls for me to come to the kitchen.

I recoil slightly at the sight and sour smell of the grey gunk Ulrike is adding to a small amount of rye flour in a very large plastic tub. It's bread starter, a bit of bread mixture left over from her last baking day. It's full of bacteria, apparently, and has been reproducing itself in this way for years. She adds warm water, I stir it into the flour, and for now that's it. I was hoping there'd be more to it, that I'd get to spend the whole afternoon pottering in the kitchen. But, unlike the dried yeast I'm used to, this dull grey mass needs a lot of time.

'Tomorrow,' Ulrike says, 'it will be bubbling with the life.'

~

Ulrike's bread has made a deep impression – Aidan shudders at the mention of it, but the rest of us find solace in its sour taste, the al dente resistance of sunflower seeds, the hint of coriander. For me, it's the centre of everything at *Il Mulino*. It's as if all the hard work is only possible because of the sustenance it provides, and every meal is drawn out around the extra slices we each take when our plates are empty. It's the staple that holds everything together and makes life on this farm particularly good. I've been looking forward to this day all week.

The kitchen has become so familiar. Its worn wooden table and heavy mismatched chairs where we gather to eat three times a day, its heirloom cabinet full of plain cracked crockery, a small bar fridge with broken shelves, the new oven and ancient sink. And, right at the back, near the fireplace that bellows black smoke inside and out, a threadbare two-seater lounge where Ulrike sometimes retires for her repose. There has never been any reason to move beyond it, until today.

The house is built on sloping land and solid timber stairs lead internally down from the kitchen to a cellar, which has its own access to the garden. The cellar is full of bottles and jars and junk. As well as producing honey, Stefan and Ulrike distil olive oil, juice apples and make honey vinegar. Hundreds of litres of each stand uniformly on crowded shelves, or haphazardly on the rough concrete floor.

On a table just inside the cellar door there's a small electric mill. Ulrike shows me where to get the wholegrain rye and the coriander seeds, and then instructs me in the art of milling. It's slow, even with the modern twist of electricity. Grain needs to be added to the mill in small batches and occasionally encouraged towards the grinding mechanism. It's a task that requires patience. She gets me a chair and suggests I might like to put it just outside the door, where I can see the garden. 'A time to think about other things,' Ulrike says.

I approach the mill with the same desire for time efficiency that dogs every other aspect of my life. The first small batch of grain falls like sand through an hourglass, a thin stream of flour slowly filling an old honey jar. It's excruciating. The second batch is a little larger, and I agitate it with my finger to speed up the process. The third batch fills the reservoir almost to the top. I add a regular shake of the mill to the finger action and perceive a slight increase in the volume of flour falling into the jar. I'm pleased with my progress, but wondering when I'll get to sit on the chair and contemplate the garden.

Overworked, the mill strains and coughs. Ulrike tells me it has overheated and needs to rest. She redirects me to the laundry to iron sheets. As I walk past the chair I kick it in the leg.

An hour later, I turn the mill back on and fill it halfway – there will be no hurrying this time.

Milling the rye, I realise, is an opportunity for repose, so I pull the chair further into the sun. It bears me no grudge for the kick and takes my weight with grace. I can see the three older children playing on a swing hanging from the cherry tree. I can't remember when I last sat to watch the children play. Aidan is standing on a chair so he can start from the highest point possible. When he jumps, the chair falls back with the force of his take-off. Marta quickly removes it from the path of the swing, and Aidan undulates his body to gain more and more height. The branch is very high, and the rope is terribly long, so Aidan flies – like Peter Pan, I think. My heart pounds with the thrill and the fear of it; any moment now he might leave that swing and either crash to the ground or fly to Neverland.

My last bowl of flour is ready to be taken to the kitchen. I've lost track of time but decide not to look at my watch (I'd like to take it off and pack it away, but its hold on me is still tight).

Ulrike is not the territorial kind. She's quite happy to sit back and give vague instructions, not fussing around the bench or scrutinising my quantities. The bread starter has grown, and its sourness hits a more pleasant note than before. Milled flour and coriander go in, sunflower seeds and linseeds, a few oats ('however the amount you like'), salt and warm water. There is mixture for seven loaves of bread, enough for the whole week. I'm nervous about getting it wrong. When I ask if I should add more water, Ulrike does one of those sideways shakes of her head, not a yes, or a no.

'Maybe. You want it not too wet, just sloppy'.

What's the difference? In the absence of disapproval, I keep guessing. When my arms can't stir anymore, Ulrike pulls a heavy electric cake mixer from the cupboard and attaches a dough hook.

'It makes better bread, and it is easier. It was worth the money.'

I agree, and my arms agree. Working in small batches, it takes nearly an hour to mix the ten kilos of dough to the right consistency. I half-fill seven large bread tins with the sloppy – perhaps slightly too wet – mixture, cover them, and take them out to sit in the sun for four hours.

'Sit with them,' she says.

'Would you like a cup of tea?' I ask

'Yes, now is a good time for tea.'

The blackened bread tins are already warm when Ulrike and I place our mugs of tea beside them. Until now, all our conversations have been about the farm and the work we're doing. Occasional forays into our children's lives have focused on school and how it's possible to take the boys away from it for so long. She seems shy, or perhaps guarded. I'm trying to imagine what it would be like to have a constant stream of

WWOOFers through your home. The effort of keeping up social graces during every meal and activity for months at a time would wear me down. When do they argue? When do they cry? When do they muck around and do things you only do in the privacy of your own home? Ulrike has closed her eyes and tilted her head towards the sun. Repose comes so easily to her. I stop thinking and follow her example. Our tea goes cold.

Ulrike doesn't mind cold tea. She's happy to sip and sit a little longer, happy to talk. She tells me about the last time she and Stefan went on holiday, and I realise she's not so different to any woman I know. It was a surprise for his birthday, a cruise, a week away from the hard work of the farm that she had saved a long time for. She made him wear nice clothes, and he hated it.

'I wanted to do something special. I need to do nice things sometimes, but he is happy here. He doesn't need anything else.'

We have one of those conversations I have every now and then, sitting in a cafe with a friend on my day off, just after we've dropped the kids at school and before we do the shopping. Ulrike and I are laughing, at ourselves and the men we love. A small shift seems to have occurred and I feel like I've been invited in.

'Is there anything I can do to help with lunch?' I ask.

Ulrike is taking our mugs back to the kitchen. 'If you can pick two lettuces from the greenhouse and wash them. We will have lunch at two.'

It's an easy job and I have two hours to do it. I follow Ulrike into the kitchen and put the kettle on to boil again. I'm feeling confident that another cup of tea will not be seen as malingering

– that was my work ethic, not hers. This is baking day, I realise: as long as a warm loaf graces the table at the end of it, I can spend the rest of my time as I wish. I fill two cups, and head down to the herb garden to sit with Shannon.

Eventually seven warm tins are brought into the kitchen, and Ulrike is telling me they'll need about one-and-a-half hours in the oven, maybe more. She's going out for coffee with a friend and will be away for the rest of the afternoon. I'm surprised. First that she'd trust me to cook the week's bread, but mostly that she has coffee with friends. For some reason it's a relief.

I put the first four tins into the hot oven and check the time on my watch. I have at least three hours to do nothing other than take these loaves out of the oven and put the remaining loaves in. The boys are with Marta down by the river, Simona has taken Amalie with her to work and everyone else is busy doing other things in other places. I have the kitchen to myself. Even here, it's a delicious thought.

I retrieve my notebook. It still feels new, full of possibility. There are a few half-page accounts of whole days, snippets of thoughts and barely formed ideas. I've been gathering recipes in the back and the odd gardening tip. I turn to a clean page, always a small thrill, and write the date in the top right-hand corner. Aidan on the swing flies onto the paper, my freshest memory.

This is my version of repose, I've decided. The capturing of moments and marshalling of thoughts calms me, and the hours ahead feel like a gift. The oven hums in the background and I lose myself to the flow of words. Then something stops my pen.

There's a change in the atmosphere that I can't quite put my finger on; there's no commotion outside, and no one has come into the kitchen. It's perfectly quiet. Too quiet. The oven has stopped humming. I look at my watch; just half an hour has passed.

I get up to check the oven, unable to calm the rising anxiety that a week's worth of bread, all that effort and ten kilos of good-quality grain, might be wasted because of my incompetence.

Nothing I do will turn the oven back on and a frantic search of the kitchen drawers fails to reveal the instruction manual. What were they thinking, putting a WWOOFer in charge of the bread? A cake, maybe, we could all live without afternoon tea, but their daily bread?

It's my fault. 'I bake at home,' I told them. I wanted so much to be useful that I convinced them I would be. I talked myself up like any would-be candidate for a project management job. I press more buttons, turn more dials. Still the oven stays silent. I'm reluctant to open it and lose whatever heat it holds, but some irrational part of me is hoping the loaves might be cooked. They're not, how could they be? An hour and half, Ulrike said. They're as pale as when they went in and the consistency of playdough. I need to find Stefan.

Luckily for me, he's not too far from the house. He and Shannon are stripping bark off the trunks of felled chestnut trees to make fence posts. As I approach I hear their voices, taking turns. Whenever Shannon speaks, Stefan turns to look at him, his hands still in motion. I'm loath to interrupt (and I'm reluctant to admit defeat), but I have to.

If Stefan's annoyed, it doesn't show. We walk towards the house, more slowly than I'm comfortable with, but when we get there he has no idea how the oven works.

'It's new,' he says.

I don't think that's the reason he can't use it, but his ignorance takes the edge off my panic. We've tried everything and have ended up doing what anyone would do in this situation: standing side by side, our hands cupping our chins, looking at the oven and waiting for an inspirational idea or a miracle. It works. The oven turns itself back on with no intervention from us, and I have an undeniable urge to hug this man who has shared my ordeal. I lean in but suddenly feel shy and the hug is aborted. There's an awkward moment, then he goes back to stripping chestnut.

Every half an hour or so the oven repeats its temperamental shut down and reboot. It completely messes with my timing, and leaves no room for repose, but I no longer think it will defeat me.

After two hours I start testing the loaves, tapping the bottom, listening for the hollow sound that apparently indicates the loaf is cooked. I've never really known what that 'hollow sound' should actually sound like, and many a hollow-sounding loaf has ended up in the compost. Stefan frequently returns to the kitchen, uncharacteristically concerned. If I fail, he'll have to endure Italian white for a whole week.

'I don't think the colour is good,' he says. 'A bit pale. Maybe ten more minutes.'

This is how we pass the afternoon, through two batches of baking. When Ulrike returns from town (a loaf of white explained away as a treat for Marta and Aidan), there are seven variously cooked loaves of rye bread filling the kitchen with their glorious aroma. Some are paler than others – they could have done with a little extra cooking – but it's decided that time will dry their doughy centres and they're put aside to be eaten later in the week. I take a slice from the best-coloured loaf and hand it to Stefan. His grin warms me, and declares the whole experiment a success.

~

A few days later honey spills, a slick translucent gold, all over my lap and shoes. It creeps under my chair and across the floor, towards a pile of broken sheets of yellow wax.

My job, earlier today, was to melt each sheet of wax, ever so gently, onto a rectangular frame strung with fine wire. The frame will eventually end up in a hive and become a scaffold for honeycomb, but first it had to be assembled. Ulrike showed me how. She was clear and unhurried, and the task took less than ten seconds. All I had to do was lay a wax sheet on the wire of a frame and heat the wire with a small electric current until the wax sank, just a little, onto it. That was the theory. But ten sheets of wax melted straight through before I began to get a feel for it. And after I got a feel for it, I still only had a success rate of around 60 per cent.

The good frames, where the wire had been swallowed by the wax but not spat out the other side, were placed one on top of the other, ready to become receptacles of sweetness in the hives. A growing sense of achievement spurred me on, my production rate increased and the bench became crowded with high-rises.

Now I have a new job in the honey room and it's another shaky start. Ulrike is smiling, her head bobbing from side to side in that way I'm beginning to think means 'don't worry'.

'The honey is warm,' she says. 'It will pour very quickly. You must release the valve only a little, like this.' She takes an empty jar and holds it under the valve of the fifty-litre vat, then barely releases the wing-nut. Honey ribbons out. The jar fills and just before it reaches the top Ulrike stops the flow.

Again, honey spills from my jar, but I see an opportunity. I summon Riley.

'Feel like a bit of honey, honey?' I say.

Small expert fingers excavate the sweet veneer on the table, odd jars are put beneath drips, the pool of honey in my lap is spooned up and swallowed. Ulrike tells him he can keep the honey he collects, so he makes a concerted effort to scrape every last drop off my trousers and arms. I try to think when I last washed either, and make a mental note to weed that jar from the collection.

'Can I stop now? I'm feeling a bit yucky,' Riley says eventually. He has filled four small jars and consumed just as much. I picture the flush of colour rising up his neck as a wave of vomit. There's already enough to clean up in here, so I deliver a quick instruction to run along and get some fresh air. He takes up his treasure and leaves me with a mop and sponge and a sweet feeling that has nothing to do with the honey still on my lips.

I hold the wing nut, and take a deep breath. The smallest twist and honey bulges through. I catch it. After a few jars I feel I've tamed it. A few more and I barely need to think about what I'm doing; my mind is free to wander. This is it, I think. This is what a good life looks like. I've spent the day as busy as a bee but still available for whatever joy presents itself. I've put lots of honey in lots of jars and in a few days Ulrike will take these jars to market and people will buy them. They'll spread the honey on their bread, stir it into their porridge, eat it by the spoonful and it will sustain them in body and in soul. I feel like I've been part of something real – I want to bottle it and take it home.

By the end of the day my sticky clothes are soaking, and Simona and I sit on the steps leading up to the kitchen. We're talking about birth while we wait for dinner.

'I was alone,' she says. 'Stefan and Ulrike were in Germany, I was here with no one, it was snow everywhere. A neighbour drove me to hospital.'

I have a crush on Simona, a desire to be around her, to impress. My middle-aged self wants her to grab hold of my hand and pull me back to my youth. It's a bit pathetic, but most crushes are. Simona was twenty-two when she gave birth to Amalie. Motherhood bridges the age gap, but it's a narrow bridge. The more I know of her the more I admire. Over the past week I've noticed her patience – with Amalie, with the work that tires her and disagreements with her parents or siblings. Italy has woeful welfare provisions for single mothers so she works harder than a young mother should have to, but she always has the energy to talk, to run along the trails through the woods, to go out with friends. Twice while we've been here, she's changed from the clothes she cleans and cares in, darkened her eyelids and left Amalie with Marta for the night.

'I go dancing in Rassina,' she says. 'Do you like to dance?'

'I do,' I say, 'I used to be in a belly dance troupe.'

Simona looks genuinely impressed and her whole body turns towards me, 'Maybe, after dinner, we can meet in the woodhouse and you can teach me.'

That wasn't the response I expected and I'm caught in a trap of my own making. I have an image of myself the last time I danced with my troupe, seven months pregnant with Riley. I was huge and prone to sciatica unless I wore a wide elasticated stabilising belt around my pelvis. A bare midriff was clearly out of the question, so I'd more or less cut a hole in a huge square of green velvet, put my head through it and tied a belt around my hips – sexy? Definitely not. The stabilising belt wasn't up to the exaggerated figure eights I had to perform in order to accommodate my velvet tent and belly overhang, and I needed help coming off the small stage set up for that particular festival. An unworthy end to a truly liberating pastime. And really, that's all it was. My little troupe was short-lived, and we danced mainly at fetes, for free, but it was transporting. I can't believe it's been nine years.

Simona is looking at me like I've danced for the queen of Egypt.

'Well, it's been a while. Since the boys were born I ...' I can't bear to say no, not because it will disappoint Simona, but because, right at this moment, I know it will disappoint me.

'I'd love that,' I say instead. Then I excuse myself, saying I need to check on the boys, and I spend the half-hour before dinner practising hip drops and belly rolls and wishing I hadn't eaten so much gelato while we were in Rome.

The woodhouse is as we left it, though there's a dank smell that I think might be coming from the mattress we dragged from under Giovanni's yurt. We haul it up and lean it against the wall. The space is small, but there's room to dance.

Simona has brought her CD player, a few scarves with coins sewn around their edges and enthusiasm. In leggings and a bikini top, she's lovely. I'm feeling like mutton dressed as lamb. I've worn a long skirt and tied my t-shirt in a knot just below my breasts, a little closer to my belly button than I would like to admit. She hands me a scarf and the tinny jingle stirs my hips into a gentle sway – they have a memory all their own.

Simona is a good belly dancer, and I feel a bit foolish trying to teach her new movements. If she's disappointed that I'm not better she masks it by politely asking me to repeat instructions. Her stomach is taut, with no sign it's carried a baby to bursting. I show her how to do belly rolls, my skin trembling above the muscular wave that moves beneath it. I used to be good at this, and before Aidan came along I sometimes imagined winning the applause of a sit-down audience. After Aidan came along I considered it an exotic workout. Now, I'm straining with the effort. Holding my stomach in is probably adding an unnecessary degree of difficulty, but I'm too vain to let it go.

There is no trembling in Simona's skin. Her belly roll is smooth and undulating, like a clean sheet hanging on the line, caressing a passing breeze. The lesson ends. *Tum tum tucka tum,* the beat of an Arabic drum fills the woodhouse. We dance.

It's close to midnight when I trip down the familiar path to the apartment. Muscles I haven't used for years have warmed and woken, and memories of myself before motherhood have been roused. It's as if I have come across something I'd forgotten was lost. I'm so pleased to have it back, but not quite sure where to put it amongst the clutter that has accumulated since.

~

Friends and family gathered around a large rustic table laden with food – this is the image that drew us, like pilgrims, to the Italian countryside.

Since arriving at *Il Mulino* we've sat around a rustic table three times a day. Friends and family pass around Ulrike's bread, her pasta or stew, salad picked fresh from the garden. We talk in three languages about the small things that matter – how to prune raspberry canes – and the big things that don't – Berlusconi's latest scandal. We reveal ourselves in increments. After only three weeks, we know each other, and I think we might know ourselves a little better too.

That is what eating good food with other people can do. Multiple courses and second helpings make us linger, and they lubricate the tongue. When we share food we indulge more than one appetite – we've sat around this kitchen table and shared knowledge, solved problems, generated ideas, relieved anxieties and confusions. The only thing left to simmer is the stew. So many people only get to experience this at Christmas, where the feast would not be complete without some social rupture that leaves the food uneaten and the cook crying into her napkin. But I wonder if that sort of thing would happen if the feasting was more regular, the problems and resentments dealt with bit by little bit?

On our last night at *Il Mulino* another feast is planned, one that Ulrike will not have to prepare. It's her fifty-fifth birthday, and Simona and Giovanni have spent the day making pasta and cooking venison and chicken in the wood-fired oven beside the house. We're looking forward to the protein.

Twenty people will gather to celebrate, so the outdoor table and an old door on a trestle are brought end-to-end on the lawn below the cherry tree. Every plate and fork in the kitchen is needed, and it's my job to gather them up and put them in their places. None of the cutlery matches, and few of the plates have escaped injury over their long lives. For three weeks I've been filling a cracked plastic salad bowl with lettuce every night, and mopping up the pool of water left behind when I clear the table after our meal. If I'd had my way a few weeks ago, that bowl would have found an alternative home in landfill then been replaced by something more durable and undoubtedly more expensive. But as I lay out each chipped plate with a mismatched knife and fork, I embrace the challenge of finding the perfect place on the table for the salad bowl: somewhere that will contain the leak rather than send it dripping onto someone's lap. I make a small internal adjustment and admit something I've been wilfully ignoring for a while now: the good life is messy and chipped, and if we do it properly there'll be no place for the aesthetic order I drool over in *Country Life*. But the compromise seems worth it; for the good food, the time and the company, a few chipped plates can be tolerated. Another lesson is noted and stored away.

At dinner Ulrike is at the head of the table, diminished by the folding chair that sits her lower than the rest of us. She knows how to relax, and I see none of the restlessness I usually feel as a host when I've been relieved of my duties. She sips from a glass of wine, the first I've seen in her hand in three weeks. I'm already on my second and hoping the few bottles on the table don't run out before I get to my third.

Simona is trying to explain to Aidan what meat makes up the *ragù* on the pasta she's piling onto his plate. His mouth gapes in horror as a childhood memory is spliced with the rich smell of meat sauce.

'"Bambi", I think you call it.'

Now he's laughing and shouting across to Riley, 'Guess what's on the pasta?'

'Bolognese?'

'No, Bambi!'

I look over at Stefan. I've poured my third glass of wine and the night is lit by the orange glow of candles. At times like this, I'm prone to fancy. He looks up and catches my gaze like he would my hand – courteous, but with a gentle caress, imperceptible to the observer, but deeply felt. I will miss him.

~

The next day we stand expectantly, arranged more or less as we were on our first morning.

Stefan has agreed to take us to the station at Rassina where we'll get a train to Florence, then to Rome, then to Naples. But first we have to say goodbye.

After three weeks, Marta, Aidan and Riley have become independent of our skirts, but they're still shy about speaking each other's languages. Riley's been making a conscientious effort, trying the sounds of new words and asking how to say important things in Italian, like 'football' and 'cricket'. He even found an old Italian–German dictionary on the bookshelves in our apartment and began translating the few Italian words he knows into German, occasionally trying them out at the dinner table. Marta would respond with one of her half-smiles and a few whispered words to her mum, before turning her gaze on Riley – the reward for his efforts.

We've worked hard during our stay at *Il Mulino*, far more hours than the WWOOFing guide suggests. At first it was because we were never told when to stop and had assumed that meant we should keep on going. After a week we realised that we could probably stop any time we liked. But whenever we saw Stefan and Ulrike, they were working. We felt obliged to help them out, simply because we could – there was no housework to catch up on, no bills to pay, no phone calls to return or meals to organise. We were time rich, and so we donated some to the cause of *Il Mulino*. Initially it was out of obligation, then out of a desire to make the hard lives of these good people a little easier, and finally because it felt good.

Stefan takes Shannon's right hand with both of his own. He doesn't shake in the usual sense, just holds.

'If you need anything, if you are in trouble or stuck, you call us. We are like your family in Italy, we will help.'

It's hard to believe we're leaving. Just before going to bed last night we all agreed that we could easily stay for months. We've become comfortable, each with our own routine intersecting with the others' throughout the long days, not just at the beginning and the end. Even the boys, with nothing in particular to do, have found some natural rhythm to replace the imposition of a school day, 'I could live like this forever,' Aidan had said. But plans have been made: another farm is expecting us in a week, and there are volcanos to climb and ancient cities to explore.

Ulrike and I hug. This reserved and guarded woman, who I've grown to admire and relate to in so many ways, says she will miss me. I know she doesn't say this to all her WWOOFers, and I hold her tighter and longer than she probably feels comfortable with. The space this family will take up in our story will be far greater than the space we take up in theirs. We're just four people out of a hundred that they'll host over the years, but they're our first. You always remember your first.

The Amalfi Coast
(Friends and fancies)

The train from Rome to Naples idles at the platform. Its interior is humid, and something fetid is wafting through the carriage. The pong has a familiar note; I look to Aidan and Riley with a raised eyebrow and quick flare of the nostrils, but they shake their heads. The boys are prone to brag about rather than deny the disgusting, so I attribute the stench to the train toilet and decide not to drink anything in the hope of avoiding it over the next few hours. It's taken us the best part of the day to get this far and we have all afternoon to go. Thank goodness there's a beach at the end of this journey.

As the train slides out of the station a man makes his way through the crush of people in the carriage. He places notes on the windowsill of each seat. They're written in English on one side, Italian on the other. A sophisticated fragrance lingers in his wake. I'm surprised when I read his note – it appears that this well-groomed man can't find work and needs money to feed his three children. I dig around in my bag for change, but then it occurs to me that this beggar might be playing us tourists for fools – how many people on the poverty line can afford expensive cologne? When he passes through the carriage the second time, I look away like everyone else.

Then I remember the perfume shop in Arezzo.

We were looking for gelato when I saw a perfumery and asked the boys, big and small, to wait. I entered the shop and pretended to browse the shelves with the intention to buy. One bottle after another was held up to my nose while I scanned the shelves. A cursory sniff of No. 19, a casual caress of Coco. I was stalking my prey. I picked up the familiar white box of Chanel No. 5 and checked the underside for a price. I moved my mouth, tilted my head, as if thinking, *Well, fifty euros isn't bad, but I wonder if I should try something else this summer, perhaps the new scent from Gucci?* I raised the tester to my nose, then, with a quick look left and right, I sprayed – wrists, neck, the full length of my scarf and as much as I could on my shirt.

I wanted the perfume to obliterate all the other smells in my clothes and skin. I hoped it would last for days, I prayed it would last for weeks, I fantasised that it would impregnate my backpack and lend a sweetness to my filthy clothes for the entire duration of our trip. Alas, it was no match for our 'woodhouse' existence, and after a day the magic had worn off.

I realise now that the beggar I shunned could easily have entered a similar shop and done the same thing. My conscience clouds.

But the perfumed man is just the first. The train stops regularly to take on its transient workforce. A woman, dressed for a day in the office, is supporting her invalid mother and younger siblings. A young man wants to work but can't. Then another woman. She looks about my age, but having fewer choices has dulled her eyes and bent her back. I watch as her gently extended hand is ignored by one passenger after another. Not once does her face register disappointment. An older man, wearing a suit and reading the paper, sees her approach. He folds the paper and searches his pockets. She stops, but it's as if she's reached the end of her leash and lost the urge to fight it – she'll take what scraps are offered then turn back. The man produces a few coins and places them in her hand along with some words I can't understand. Without raising her head, she thanks him in Italian, though the accent is strange.

The most striking thing about the whole exchange is her complete lack of expression and the downward tilt of her head; her gaze seems fixed to a point on the ground that is just one step ahead. She's been doing this a long time, and a few coins aren't going to save her.

When she arrives at our seats I drop the coins I've been holding into her hand. I try to catch her eye, but that's not part of the deal – two Euros doesn't buy me recognition. What, after all, have I actually done?

An hour later, the open windows bring a breeze and the smell of acacia blossom. Stefan's bees will now be busy making the glassy-gold honey that Riley was so fond of at *Il Mulino*. Their invitation to come back in June to help with the honey harvest made it easier to leave, and for a few minutes I indulge in thoughts of Stefan and his generous way of seeing the world.

~

In Naples, we run to catch the afternoon commuter train and squeeze in for the final stage of our long day. A corridor of food – lemon trees and vegetable gardens – ushers us around the Bay of Naples towards the seaside town of Sorrento. Summer will bring a torrent of Northern Europeans, but now, in early May, it should be relatively quiet. Mount Vesuvius plays peek-a-boo behind the urban sprawl, and Aidan bounces in his seat. Vesuvius captured his imagination when he did a project on volcanos in Year Five – its dormant temper and destructive outburst became the catalyst for many homemade eruptions involving vinegar, baking soda and red food colouring. As a drawcard, it came a close second to gelato.

We pass *Pompei Scavi*, the station where we'll get off when we visit Pompeii, and suddenly I feel we're on holiday again – five lazy days of sightseeing and coastal loitering, gelato and pastries. Not a single weed will come between us and the pleasures of the Amalfi Coast. When we finally stop, my optimism has just about extinguished the exhaustion of ten hours of train hopping, and I bound out of the station with the boys trotting to keep up.

'Shall we try to find a room with a view of Vesuvius?' I ask them.

'We might be lucky to find a room with a view of anything,' Shannon says. 'Look.' It's late afternoon, and the streets fanning out from the station are crowded with holiday makers. 'It looks like we've arrived right in the middle of seniors' week.'

Optimism turns to panic – we haven't booked anywhere to stay. We consult our guidebook, make enquires at every hotel between the station and the town, line up at visitor information and make call after call until our cheap prepaid mobile sends us a message in Italian that Shannon thinks is a warning that our credit is low. All the budget places are fully booked; all the mid-range places are fully booked. The only rooms available have a view over the bay, but one night would cost the equivalent of our gelato budget for the whole trip – it's not an option. Three hours after arriving we still have nowhere to sleep, and Sorrento has taken on the character of a New Year's Eve party. The bars are overflowing and the streets are teeming with people in their holiday best, talking and laughing and stopping to peruse menus. Shannon is dispatched to look further afield.

'Hang in there, boys,' I say, once Shannon has gone. They've been dragged from hotel to hotel, their grumbles silenced with Sprite and gelato, and now they're perched on top of our packs, absorbed in their DS games. They don't acknowledge my encouragement, but I let it go. As much as I hate these gadgets there's no denying their qualities of distraction.

The last time I was in Italy and couldn't find accommodation to suit my impoverished budget, I made my way back to the train station and set up camp in front of a closed-up shop. I was with a friend, and we considered it an adventure. But the prostitutes and the dealers and the woman with leprosy are not what I want my boys to remember about our holiday on the Amalfi Coast.

I overhear an elderly couple from Liverpool discussing where to have dinner and imagine asking if they'd mind taking my children to sleep on their hotel floor: 'They can be delightful company,' I'd say. Just as I'm about to approach them, Shannon comes back from his search beyond the town. The news is mediocre.

'No rooms anywhere, but I found a number on a notice board.'

I press the numbers into our phone in the sluggish manner of someone who knows it's a waste of effort. It connects. A cheery man answers and I say the only phrase I'm fluent in, '*Mi dispiace, non parlo italiano. Parli inglese?*'

'*Sì, sì, signora*, I speak English.'

Despite this reassurance, I fail to understand half of what he says. But I'm sixty per cent sure he has a room for four, and that it's well within our meagre budget. I say we'll be there soon and hang up.

When we get to the hotel it's clear I've misunderstood the price, but exhaustion from the long walk out of town and an image of my children watching an old woman remove bandages from her leprous legs just before they fall asleep on platform one have increased the value of a roof and a bed. I didn't have a credit card when I was eighteen, but I do now – I hand it over and take the key.

Our cabin is hidden in a lemon grove. We stand on the verandah and embrace each other in that giddy way you do when misfortune passes you by. Then we hear a muffled voice. It's Riley, he's squashed in the middle of our family hug.

'Can we have dinner soon?' he asks. It was forgotten during our search for accommodation.

'I know just the thing,' I say.

Shrivelled and small, the truffle is hardly inspiring, and now I have it in my hand I'm not sure what to do with it. I decide that less-is-more and simple-is-best, and put a pot of water on to boil – it's always a good place to start.

But when the pasta is nearly ready I'm still uncertain. Too many expectations have been wrapped around this pungent prize. Every time we unzipped the pack, the truffle's odour – damp and organic – would tease my mouth and make it water. Shannon had to stop me flinging T-shirts, socks and underpants to the floor. 'Patience,' he'd say, 'think how much you'll enjoy it if you wait.'

Well, I've waited. Tonight's the night. And I have performance anxiety. I pick it up – it feels lighter than I remember. I bring it to my nose – nothing. That can't be right. I repeat the gesture, sniff harder, but my mouth does not water.

The pasta is ready, the truffle untouched. I fuss with a colander, drizzle some oil, reach for a vegetable peeler. The resistant outer layer is eventually shed revealing marbled flesh – white veins through black.

Steam rises from the pasta and I shave the truffle into it. Toss, taste. It's bland. A bit of salt, a pinch of pepper, some more truffle. Taste. Still bland. More salt, more pepper – I haven't got much to work with. It tastes a bit salty, a bit peppery, but not very much like truffle.

'I don't know why it's so expensive, it barely has any flavour.' Shannon is unimpressed.

'It usually does, but I think all the flavour has been absorbed into our clothes.'

Luckily, we have a box full of cake and pastries. I eat two helpings of tiramisu and resolve never again to think of the truffle.

~

Over the next few days we dawdle along the congested lanes of Sorrento, run our hands through racks of T-shirts, pick up knick-knacks and thingamajigs and make disparaging remarks about the people who buy them. We eat gelato and pastries, find a thingamajig we can't resist and buy it. We do everything together, so when the boys beg to go into a lolly shop that's right next door to a women's clothing store, I'm quick to agree.

'Of course. Here's two euros each. Take your time.' With a kiss for each we see them safely into the lolly shop then Shannon disappears into the lanes and I enter the hallowed space of the ladies' boutique.

I want a hat. Mine has been left behind in Stefan's van. Since realising its absence, I've imagined, on more than one occasion, that Stefan will come across it while unloading his hives and stop for a minute to remember me – I see his smile, and the small sideways tilt of his head. When he brings the hat to his face to inhale my scent, the image becomes a bit fuzzy – this isn't something Stefan would do and, frustratingly, my imagination refuses to fully cooperate.

I'm tossing up between a practical canvas hat and a large straw hat with a floppy, oversized brim. The canvas one would serve me well when I'm weeding or planting or whatever else I'll be doing at the next few farms, but the straw hat, matched with the Jackie O sunglasses I bought in Rome, makes me look a bit like a European aristocrat holidaying on the Amalfi Coast. I'm still thinking about it when I hear the boys come into the shop. I fear their sticky fingers around all the white linen shirts I can't afford and realise I need to make a quick decision. When I race out of the change room to claim my children, it's the less than practical straw hat I put on the counter.

We find Shannon in a small park on the edge of the cliff that supports the town.

'Is that Mt Vesuvius?' Riley asks.

'Sure is,' Shannon says.

The people of *Surrentum*, as Sorrento was called in Roman times, would have had a spectacular view of the erupting Vesuvius. It rises from the Bay of Naples, dark and looming, a dense skirt of humanity clinging to its base – a puzzle, given it could erupt again with equal violence. Shannon points out the general location of Pompeii.

'We'll go there tomorrow.' he says.

'Then can we climb the volcano?' asks Aidan.

'Absolutely,' I say, with more enthusiasm than I actually feel.

The boys lean over the stone balustrade, the only thing between them and the bay. I suspect their imaginations are animating Vesuvius with lava flows and a crown of smoke and flame. The drum of an explosion fills my ears, but it's only one of those three-wheeled vehicles, a load of crates with empty bottles, shaking over the cobbled road.

After dinner I stand between the boys and the television reading passages from our guidebook and quizzing them on the details.

'Who can tell me when Mount Vesuvius exploded and buried Pompeii and Herculaneum?'

'Muuuum. Coyote was just about to get Road Runner,' says Aidan.

'Coyote never gets Road Runner, no matter what language it's in. Come on, when did Vesuvius erupt?'

'Seventy-nine AD.'

At this moment I see Aidan graduating from university, a degree in volcanology in his hand, a speech of thanks to Shannon and me for taking him to Vesuvius when he was twelve, walking with him among the ruins of Pompeii and opening his eyes to the power of nature over humanity. I'm not sure you can get a degree in volcanology, and I'm pretty sure that graduates don't give speeches, but I have high hopes that the next few days will plant seeds of interest that might flourish into meaningful careers.

'Now can you move?' he says.

Then again, he might become a cartoonist.

~

81

Pompeii and Vesuvius have been enjoyed and suffered, depending on your perspective: we now have three kilos of volcanic rock to cart around in our packs, and my favourite jeans are a bit worse for wear after I lost my footing and slid down the volcano on my bum – a particular highlight for the boys. There were other highlights, glimpsed through the crowds, but not as many as we'd hoped. What impressed us most was evidence that our life is not so different to the lives of people living thousands of years ago – a mosaic warning visitors to 'beware of the dog', an ancient take-away food store, a bakery with a wood-fired oven big enough for all of us to sit inside (I wondered if they'd called their bread 'artisan'). Then there was a wisp of sulphur rising from the crater of Vesuvius. When the boys started to throw rocks at it I told them to stop in case the volcano woke up. They laughed and redoubled their efforts. Despite seeing the final terror of adults and children preserved in stone, they couldn't imagine any such tragedy befalling them.

Now, on the last day of our stay on the Amalfi Coast, I'm sitting on the floor of the bus we're on in an effort to stop myself from vomiting – there's less lurch down here. Apparently the view is incredible, but I really couldn't care less. For forty-five minutes we've hugged the contours of the coast, like a roller coaster hugs its rails. When the bus stops I escape with a dozen other green-gilled passengers and spend a few minutes sucking in the sea air.

Our guide book describes Positano as 'the coast's most photogenic and expensive town'. It clings to the side of a cliff, crowded and colourful, its lowest buildings almost touching the blue of the sea. When I recover enough to look up, I see a postcard image. Boutique shops line one side of the steep road leading down to the town's centre, and tourists taking selfies line the other. I put on my big sunglasses and adjust my floppy hat.

'Let's ask someone to take a photo,' I say to Shannon.

He rolls his eyes and lets out an exaggerated groan; I have form when it comes to passing our camera to unsuspecting strangers.

My family stands, resigned. I start to stage manage. Shannon's beard has become unruly, there's nothing I can do about that. If I'd anticipated this photo, I might have suggested a visit to the barber, clean T-shirts, a face washer. I didn't, so all I can do is direct Shannon to put the day pack out of sight, tell the boys to take off their caps, and wipe gelato from the edges of Riley's mouth (I want his cooperation so I use the edge of my skirt instead of a licked thumb). When I think we're as good as we're going to get I scan the stream of tourists for someone with a real camera hanging around their neck. I'm looking for a Nikon or a Canon, the longer the lens the better. When I pass over our little camera, I want to be sure they know how to focus.

'Do you mind taking one more?' I ask the Brit with the adequate lens. 'Make sure you get a bit of the view.' The Brit is compliant, but I can feel Shannon squirming. I look obliquely towards the sea, as if contemplating an impending romance, but it's a hard posture to maintain. By the time I hear the shutter click (fake but strangely satisfying), my face has collapsed and Shannon has shouldered the pack.

The road eventually narrows and market stalls crowd the footpath. A ring with an aqua stone catches my eye, and I stop at the stall to have a closer look.

'Maybe we'll find Pokémon gelato here,' Riley says. The thought makes him impatient and I'm dragged away before I can try the ring on.

The main beach is dull and uncomfortable-looking – as former Sydney-siders we try to be generous with our coastal judgements, but the need for protective footwear always draws a harsh review. We stop for gelato (no Pokémon here either) then walk around the cliff to a smaller beach called *Spiaggia del Fornillo*.

My swimmers cover much more of my posterior than fashion dictates, and I imagine the smirks and pitying looks of those in less fabric. I quash the feeling, which is like I'm walking into a cocktail party dressed in a muumuu, and settle on a blue-and-white striped sun lounge, under a blue-and-white striped umbrella. I start reading *The History of Love* by Nicole Krauss, and when I get too hot I hobble across the pebbly beach to float in the Mediterranean – it's ridiculously blue. I tilt back my head so my ears are submerged and hear sand shifting with the current. It sounds like the breath of a sea in slumber, and I feel myself retreat, or emerge, or both if that's possible. When I come out of the water, I notice two skinny boys in hats and long sleeves. They're building a fort of sand at the water's edge. They're familiar, but for now, they don't belong to me.

I spend the next few hours as a young, childless European aristocrat with a yacht moored just off the beach and a house in Monaco. I lose track of the goings-on of the common folk, though I'm not oblivious to their attentions. On the sun lounge next to mine a bearded fellow with a farmer's tan steals glances at my naked legs when he thinks I'm not looking. It's not hard to read him: he's pretending he shares a blue-and-white striped umbrella with a gorgeous, aristocratic European in a bikini that fashionably spends most of its time up her small suntanned bottom.

I'd like to think that a little of this fantasy is real, but if I'm honest it would only be that I do, indeed, have a bottom, though it's neither small nor suntanned – who has the time to achieve either when you're not really a European aristocrat?

A woman has just shifted her sunlounge from under its umbrella and is offering her face to the sun. She's thin and bronze-breasted. Actually, her whole body is bronzed, but it's her breasts that have captured my attention. They sit neatly on her chest, wobbling slightly when she moves. There's no hint of augmentation.

In Sydney, during the 1980s, and before I had absorbed the message about skin cancer, I used to sunbathe topless. My boobs were never neat or particularly bronzed (despite lashings of baby oil), but like all seventeen-year-old breasts, they were an adequate offering to the sun. I shift my sunlounge, untie the knot around my neck and pull the top half of my swimmers to my waist. There's considerable wobble, but I'm prepared for that: it's the shock of being released from bondage, the sudden lack of support. What I don't expect is their hasty retreat from the sun. Like blind moles, their pink noses quivering, they head to ground. I look along the length of my two-toned torso, and they're nowhere to be seen. They are sheltering in the shadows of my armpits, doing nothing to bring my fantasy to life. I retrieve one, and then the other, put them back in their padded cells and re-tie the knot that anchors them in place.

My bronzed muse rises to cool off in the sea. Her breasts drop, just enough. Her bottom, I notice, is dimple free. I roll off my sunlounge and put on my ankle-length skirt.

'I'm going to explore the shops,' I tell the bearded man.

My long skirt, floppy hat and big sunglasses might be enough to hide the reach of age, so I slow to a stroll and increase the swing of my hips. I'm risking mockery, to be sure, but there's a chance that a fuller figure still has currency in this country of sensual pastimes, and I still have a fantasy to indulge.

Brown eyes follow my progress through a square behind *Spiaggia Grande*. '*Bellissima*,' their owner calls, and I rejoice in the effectiveness of my disguise. Shannon and I will laugh when I tell him. He'll pull me into him and mimic the Italian accent of my admirer. I'll invite him back to my yacht, and we'll make love.

I have good friends who understand this need for escape; they crave time alone, to think, to create, to abandon obligation, as much as I do. Before we left they presented me with a pouch of keepsakes – a small object from each to carry with me.

'We want you to have us with you, to know that we love you.'

They also gave me money with instructions to buy myself jewellery. They know about tight budgets and the guilt of spending money on personal luxuries, and had anticipated the joy I might feel browsing in the shops of an exotic place and buying something just for its beauty. I love them for this, and for so much else. I especially love that they are the kinds of friends who will laugh hysterically when they find out that when it was clear we'd packed far too much to carry, the little pouch of keepsakes was regretfully placed in a box and left in Adelaide along with two books, a pair of shoes and a dress 'for when we go out'.

I wonder now what my life would be like without these women, without their wisdom and frailty, their humour and sympathy – it would be lonelier, and less certain. I must remember to tell them when I get home.

The ring with the aqua stone is still there. The woman selling it tells me it was once a stalactite. It slides easily onto my middle finger, the stone an oasis of cool, like the Mediterranean, against the browned skin of my hand. I consult my friends – each one is a voice in my head, if not an object in my pocket.

Margi is emphatic. 'It's beautiful,' she says, 'buy it.'

Rebekah urges me to try another, then another. 'You need to be sure. This will be your touch stone – the thing that transports you back to this place when the place you are in is driving you nuts.'

Jolie waits until I have tried them all. 'It's the same colour as the water; you have no choice.'

Unfortunately, we have expensive taste. They haven't given me enough money for this ring, so I'm obliged to haggle. Each throws in her two cents' worth, Jolie reminding me that I'm paying with cash. Bek suggesting I tell the story – of them, farewell drinks in the pub, the gift of money and the pouch of keepsakes. Just when I think Margi is going to suggest that I produce the keepsakes to authenticate my story, the woman selling the ring relents.

'You have good friends. You're very lucky.' She accepts our money and places the ring on my finger. A sudden feeling of wedded bliss washes over me – I'll have these friends forever.

Calabria

(Work like an old, rusty tractor)

As the train slows I realise that I have too, and my thoughts return to Tuscany. I close my eyes and see Shannon and Stefan, so comfortable in each other's company, looking over the field that will grow vegetables in the hot months to come. They're discussing the what, when and where of planting. These decisions will initiate a sequence of activities – in the field and in the house – that will unite the family in purpose, and sustain them in body and spirit until the next time they stand looking over a field deciding what and when and where to plant. It's the rhythm of life we're looking for and I can't wait to know how it plays out on the next farm.

We're the only people getting off at Zambrone. We dump our packs on the platform and watch the train pull away. It reveals the Mediterranean, a glittering temptation.

'Can we go to the beach?' Aidan asks.

'No, not now,' I say. 'The farm isn't far, so maybe we can come down tomorrow afternoon.'

The beach was one of the reasons we chose this place. We can't afford a car, so we've tried to include farms within walking distance of things to do when we're not working. 'Twenty minutes' walk to the beach,' the farm guide said, so I arranged to stay for a month – there'll be plenty of time for swimming.

Aidan loads his pack onto his back without complaint. The sound of waves accompanies us as we leave the platform, and I call the number I've been given. Gianni answers, his accented English is warm and welcoming. '*Buongiorno*, welcome. My wife will be there very soon. She has just left.'

I'm looking forward to meeting Lauren – our shared language, the Zen missives she always puts at the ends of her emails, the fact she's living my dream. When she gets out of an old station wagon, her long cotton skirt and floral headscarf complete a picture that I want to be painted into.

We pile in. There aren't enough seatbelts, but I've learned to accept this sort of thing with a convenient 'it will never happen to me' attitude. The only time I waver is when we meet a landslide halfway up the steep and winding road to the farm. It's on a bend and blocks more than half of the road, so Lauren has to cross to the opposite side to get around it. A collective intake of breath, clenching of buttocks and anticipation of a head-on collision plays out in all our minds. If the car coming the other way is driving with the necessary caution, we might get away with minor cuts and bruises.

The car coming the other way is not driving with the necessary caution, but we've just come around the bend when it approaches. I feel we've dodged a bullet.

'When did the landslide happen?' I ask.

'Oh, about four months ago.'

'But it's so dangerous, why hasn't it been cleared?'

'Mafia. None of them live up this way, it's not a priority.'

'What have the Mafia got to do with road maintenance?'

'They're part of the *Comunale*, the local government.'

My knowledge of the Mafia comes from 1970s movies. If I think of them at all I see horses' heads in beds and dark-suited men in fedora hats. The Italy we've been travelling in seems a long way from those things, but Lauren, in a matter-of-fact way, is making it clear that the Mafia's influence is still pervasive.

She manoeuvres the station wagon through a gate and up a dirt road. Vines and vegetables are on our right; chickens can be seen through the trees on the left. The track opens up, and the station wagon comes to a stop.

We take our packs from the back of the car and stand, waiting for direction. Several two-storey buildings are scattered around, bougainvillea clambers their rendered walls, hammocks hang under their eaves. They're all turned towards the shining sea. A moment of dreaming and I can see the weight of my snoozing body giving shape to a hammock that's now hanging loose on a second-floor balcony.

The farm is called *Pirapora*. Gianni and his brother Franco grew up here, and they now live here with their families. Together they run an *agriturismo* – farm-based accommodation for tourists. They grow organic food, make organic wine, and in the summer they feed and shelter up to forty guests seeking a taste of the good life – here that's defined as home-grown food, the hot Calabrian sun and long days on the beach.

'This way,' says Lauren.

We turn our backs on the view and follow her past a large laundry room, around the back of which is the small house that she shares with Gianni and their two small children, Luca and Sophie. Beside it is our room. Both dwellings face inland, providing a behind-the-scenes look at paradise – tangled weeds and broken masonry, the beginnings of a garden bed, rows of washing-line hung with white sheets.

The room is clean, bright, airy. There's an empty cupboard, a couple of chairs, bunk beds and a double – we're expected. Shannon squeezes my hand, I squeeze back. It's a silent conversation that recalls our first day at *Il Mulino*. Lauren insists we relax for the rest of the afternoon, and we both release the breath we barely knew we were holding.

We fill empty shelves with clothes, our toilet bag and books. Aidan takes the top bunk, Riley the bottom, their teddies and DSs are carefully arranged. I automatically put my pyjamas and notebook under the pillow on the left side of the bed, Shannon puts the phone, his wallet and the iPod on the chair to the right. I realise I miss nothing from home, none of the things that fill the spaces of our house. I'm not naive enough to think we'd be happy to live like this forever, but since being in Italy, and especially at *Il Mulino*, I've realised that any efforts we've made in the past to live with less have been a bit pathetic. Actually, I think the opposite has happened. In Sydney we were constrained by a tiny house with no garage or shed. Since moving to the

Adelaide Hills we've acquired both. There are so many places to store crap that looked essential to my happiness when I saw it in the shop but turned out not to be. A couple of months ago, replacing a cracked salad bowl would have been the perfect antidote to work stress and a fine way to spend a lunch hour. But the bowl would have one salad day and end up collecting dust in the garage because it was a bit too big for our real needs (and any of our kitchen cupboards). It would be perfect for a dinner party, of course, but I'd have to remember where I'd put it.

'I love living with so few things,' I say to Shannon. 'We should hire a skip when we get home and throw out everything we haven't used in the past year.'

'Okay ...' he says, in that drawn out way that means he thinks I haven't thought it through. 'You'll get no argument from me, but I think you might have forgotten the last time we hired a skip?'

I look at him blankly while I forage around in my mind for the memory.

'We spent all day filling it with junk and you snuck back in the evening to save a whole box of useless stuff.'

It's coming back to me now. 'How did you know?'

'I found the box.'

'And what did you do with it?'

'Chucked it back in the skip.'

'But all that stuff meant something to me.'

'Pip, that was two years ago and you didn't even know it was missing.' He flops onto the bed and lies back with his hands behind his head and an expression of amused satisfaction.

It's time to change the subject. 'Shall we go for a walk?' I ask.

The goat track from our door joins a paved path that leads us to the farm restaurant. It's a large room with lots of windows and a shiny stainless steel kitchen behind swinging double doors. There's also an outdoor pizza oven, a small green lawn and a view of the volcanic island of Stromboli. It's smoking.

Stromboli is the kind of volcano a child would draw – a perfect triangle with the top sliced off and a vertical plume of smoke dividing the sky. It sits clearly on the horizon, and in the foreground the sea undulates towards the Calabrian coast. We're not the only ones captivated by the sight. A young couple sit on a bench, their gaze shifting between the volcano and their toddling daughter. Three others have paused their game of cards and stand at the edge of the garden to watch Stromboli breathe. All of them are speaking German.

'Will it erupt?' asks Riley.

'I hope so,' says Aidan, almost to himself. He's mesmerised. It's as if he's following the trace of a firework climbing into the sky – he believes something extraordinary might happen.

The couple with the baby introduce themselves, in English, as Bianca and Horst, then ask us where we're from, how long we'll be staying. There's no expectation that we should speak their language, but I still wish we'd enrolled in 'German for Fun and Travel' before our journey. Our conversation draws the others closer, turns their faces inland. We're a curiosity, and Stromboli isn't going anywhere.

'And how is it that you can take the children out of school for so long?' someone asks.

'It wasn't a problem. The teachers know they'll learn from travelling, they just asked them to keep a journal and do a bit of maths and English.'

'That is all? In Germany it could not be done, you would not be allowed.' We've heard this before – from Germans, Italians, other Europeans. They envy this freedom we have to roam with our children. Some have called us brave, hinting that there's something dangerous about stepping off the treadmill, even if only for a short time. It's as if we're breaking some societal rule. I wonder what they fear most: an unscripted life, or the possibility they'll love it but inevitably have to go back to the real world? I've feared the first, but now that we've taken the plunge I have no intention of stepping back on the treadmill when I get home, so I don't expect the second.

Others beam, wanting to know as much as we can tell. Bianca and Horst are like this.

'Do it,' I say. 'It's the best thing we've ever done as a family.' As the words come out I realise how true they are. There's nothing in the history of our family that I'm more grateful for than this time we're spending together.

'And you, Shannon. Is it something you would recommend?' Horst asks.

'It's a great experience for all of us, but mostly it's a chance to get some perspective. That's never a bad thing.'

When their daughter's tired grizzles pull them away, we wander back up the path for a rest.

~

The bell for dinner pulls us from sleep or fiction and into our new world. I look at my watch and share the good news with Shannon.

'It's only seven o clock,' I say. Our bag of emergency food won't be needed.

We amble down the path to the restaurant where we'll eat breakfast and dinner each day. Gianni's broad smile beckons us in. When I ask if there's anything we can help with he insists that tonight we do nothing. Then he points towards the back of the room. Amongst all the tables with white linen coverings, glasses for wine and water, and small vases of flowers, sits a plain wooden table, unadorned and looking a little forlorn.

'That is your table, and everything you need for eating you will find in here.' Gianni opens the doors of a large wooden cupboard to reveal all manner of crockery and cutlery and little wire baskets containing small bottles of vinegar and oil, then he leaves to check on something in the kitchen.

We lay our table with everything we think we need (no linen table cloth) then take our seats. Paying guests start to arrive. Those we didn't meet earlier look a little confused when they scan our impoverished table, while others acknowledge us with a slightly uncomfortable nod. Bianca and Horst come over and invite us to join them at their table.

'I don't think we can,' I say to them, and we arrange to catch up for a drink at the end of the meal.

The last of the guests has been served and the boys have started to complain that they're hungry, 'It's a bit *Upstairs, Downstairs*,' I whisper to Shannon.

'Maybe the waitress can't see us back here; it's pretty dim,' he says.

'Maybe we're supposed to serve ourselves,' I say.

I'm about to get up to enquire when Gianni comes out of the kitchen with a tray of food.

'After today, you can help yourselves from the kitchen,' he says. 'But now, I will serve you.'

With a huge smile he puts a basket of sourdough in the middle of the table and places a large bowl of porcini risotto in front of each of us. There is only water for the boys, but he offers Shannon and me wine or beer – both made on the farm, and tells us where we can find more if our glasses run dry.

Aidan is halfway through his risotto before Gianni has even left our table. Riley would rather eat dirty socks than anything with mushrooms in it so he pushes his bowl towards his brother and soaks a thick slice of bread in olive oil. Shannon and I try to show mature restraint, but within minutes all four bowls are empty. When Gianni notices, he comes around with the pot and refills them.

'I bet the serving classes never ate this well,' Shannon says when he finishes his second helping.

I have to agree. It looks like our lowly position in the dining room hierarchy entitles us to the leftovers. Now that I've tasted Gianni's cooking I'm not only happy to forgo a table cloth and waiter service, but I'd willingly eat sitting on the floor with a paper plate and plastic fork.

Then a second course arrives. We didn't expect it, and have filled up on bread and risotto. But we don't send it back – thick slices of eggplant, grilled and layered with homemade tomato sauce and topped with a parmesan crust: parmigiana the way it was always meant to be, and a far cry from the Thursday night special at our local pub. When I've finished what's on my plate I lean towards Riley's.

'We can't send it back untouched, sweetheart, he might be offended.' I raise a full fork to his mouth, but he clamps it shut. In a practised move, perfected during his infancy, the fork makes a U-turn and lands comfortably on my tongue. I realise I've started something I may not have the willpower to stop.

'Shannon, take the fork before I go too far.'

He takes the fork, just as Gianni delivers dessert: four hefty portions of tiramisu. A dilemma.

After my slide down Mount Vesuvius I stood in front of the mirror to examine the damage to my favourite jeans. It was little more than a smudge of dirt, but closer inspection revealed more than I expected – much more.

Shannon laughed. He was looking at me looking at my bum in the mirror, 'It looks pretty good to me,' he said.

'You always say that.'

'It always looks good.'

'Did we use hot water the last time we washed clothes?'

'Those jeans haven't seen a washing machine since we left Adelaide.'

That fact should have been the most disturbing thing about our conversation, but it wasn't. 'So why are they so tight? I can't even do them up properly.'

'It's getting warmer, you won't need to wear them soon.'

'So you agree, my bum is getting bigger?'

'Maybe a bit, but it's just more to love.'

'Right then, no more pastries, no matter how small they are. And definitely no more tiramisu.'

Now Shannon is looking at me, his smirk reminding me of my declaration. He knows it's beyond my powers to push the dessert away, but he's curious about how long it'll take me to cave in.

I stick my tongue out at him and have a small taste. It's sublime. All hope of a speedy reconciliation with my jeans is abandoned as I begin spooning it into my mouth. When I agree to seconds – or have I just crawled into the kitchen with my empty plate and begged for more? – the love I once had for my jeans becomes a distant memory, and I have to accept that it's time we go our separate ways.

Dishes done, Shannon and the boys roll me up the path to our room. We're tired, and full, and delighted. When the light goes out we chatter in the dark, tell stories about the boys from when they can't remember. They love to hear them, over and over, and we have all the time in the world to tell them. That's the gift of a shared room without a television or internet. It's a gift we've unwrapped almost every night since we arrived in Italy.

~

The morning after our arrival, we're running late.

Lauren told us last night that we were to start work at half past eight in the morning, but at half past seven I lost the soap.

One minute it was under my right armpit, the next it was in the toilet. When I leaned over the bowl to try to locate it, the water cascading off my breasts churned the surface and I couldn't see a thing. Had I flushed? I couldn't remember, but I did recall thinking there would be no point, as I'd have to flush later. The shower is located just above the toilet, an afterthought probably, but I could see its multi-task potential, and even though the time-hungry demon that lurks inside me has been tamed over the past month, I couldn't help but admire the design – until I lost the soap.

After a silent debate I took the plunge, swished my hand around in the mire and pulled out my treasure: it was soft, and a little slimy. Hoping that this was nothing more than the effects of immersion, I rinsed it until the skin on my fingers was puckered and pale. By the time I'd finished showering; dried myself; wiped down the walls, sink and toilet seat; and dressed in the mostly-dry clothes that I'd hung out the bathroom window for safe-keeping, the hour for breakfast was almost over.

Now it's just after eight, and we're sitting alone in the farm restaurant – the guests are all sleeping in. I hurry the boys to eat up, but something about my tone transports me six thousand kilometres to a place where school and work hold sway over us. *We've come too far for this*, I think, so I back off.

'What time would it be at home?' Riley asks.

'About 5.30 in the afternoon,' I say. 'I'd be stuck in traffic right now. I've probably just called someone a dingbat for not knowing how to merge.'

'That's not the word you'd use,' says Aidan.

'No, it's not,' agrees Shannon, and Aidan gives him a strawberry-jam smile.

'You guys would probably be doing homework,' I say.

'This is way better than doing homework,' Aidan says.

'What would you be doing, Dad?' Riley asks.

'Pruning our apple trees. I should have done it before we left, but I ran out of time.'

The boys get a second helping of sourdough and jam, Shannon has a second coffee, and I drizzle oil on bits of torn up mozzarella.

We amble back up to our room to find Lauren waiting and looking at her watch.

'I wanted to get down to the vines before it got too late,' she says. 'You'll need boots.'

I want, more than anything, to get on with Lauren and be privy to the secrets of her good life, so I negotiate a quick division of labour with Shannon. He already has his boots on so he'll follow Lauren while I sort out the kids. He grabs a water bottle and strides out. Lauren is halfway down the path. I look at my own watch – it's 8.25.

My resolve not to rush the kids suddenly dissolves. I'm like one of Pavlov's dogs; a ticking clock elicits an automatic panic response that involves various entreaties to the boys to 'help me out' and a whole vocabulary of small noises indicating that their efforts are not up to standard. While I tie my bootlaces I issue directives for teeth cleaning and school work, and suggest a number of other activities that might fill the five hours between now and when we stop for lunch. No DS until this afternoon, once we've checked their maths, and no fighting – we'll be too far away to save them from each other.

Shannon is half a kilometre away, near the bottom of the steep, overgrown escarpment. There's no path as far as I can see, though my search is a bit frenetic. I take a deep breath and raise my gaze from the scrub to the Mediterranean. The sea is calm around Stromboli, and she's breathing lightly, barely a wisp. How I'd love to take Aidan there. That I'm calmed by a volcano makes me laugh. I take another look for the path and there it is, right in front of me.

I slip twice and arrive at the vines panting and rubbing my bum. Shannon looks at me as if to say, 'Again? You're kidding me.' I can only shrug. Lauren is explaining that three rows of grapes need to be pulled out, a white variety that isn't suited to the climate.

'You should get all the stakes out before lunch,' she says.

Her demonstration indicates this might be ambitious: the ground is dry and hard, and the first three stakes refuse to budge. But the fourth yields, and she's convinced the rest will follow.

Just before leaving us she points towards the industrial kitchen built on the edge of the escarpment, 'I'll be up the top working in the *laboratorio*. I'll pop out every now and then to see how you're going.' She turns to go back up the slope, then stops; she has one more bit of advice. 'By the way, the escarpment has great acoustics, so be careful what you say.'

Over the next couple of hours, Shannon and I speak only in whispers.

When we finally start the climb back up, I'm nervous – the boys have been alone for nearly five hours. It's the same feeling I used to get when they were babies and had slept longer than usual; reason told me there was no need to panic, but as I walked towards the room where they slept I'd begin to sweat. My heartbeat wouldn't slow until I held them against me, warm and alive. It's like that now, and I chastise myself for not coming up to check on them earlier.

They're building Lego with Luca on the unfinished patio. They've survived our neglect. I bend to kiss their heads and slow my heart.

Shannon and I go to wash the vines and escarpment from our hands, but the soap is much reduced since the toilet fiasco and doesn't produce any lather. I go and find Lauren, who is in her tiny kitchen gathering plates and cutlery to lay the table for our lunch.

'Lauren, can we have some more soap?' I ask.

Her knitted eyebrows question why I would need more soap when she gave me a new block yesterday.

'I dropped it in the toilet,' I say.

The news doesn't seem to surprise her. She goes to the cupboard and brings out a box. Different shapes, colours and scents.

'Do you make it?' I ask.

'Carluccia taught me, Gianni's mum. She's always made her own soap. We'll be making some tomorrow if you want to help.'

When we started planning this WWOOFing life, I imagined a lot more making and a lot less weeding. I wanted our souvenirs of Italy to be knowledge and skills, not blisters and sore backs. Shannon knew better. He's closer to the daily slog of growing vegetables and keeping the weeds at bay on our own block. I remember him putting a hand gently on my shoulder as I read out descriptions of farms who listed baking and cheese-making among their activities.

'You know, Pip, it's more likely we'll be doing the hard, dirty, boring stuff.'

I declared it would be a joy to be outdoors, working with my body instead of stuck in front of a computer all day, but in truth I knew my body might not be up to it, and my mind would want for more. So I continued to imagine myself as an apprentice to Italian traditions. At *Il Mulino* I made some adjustments to the dream, so this morning's job of pulling wooden stakes from the unyielding earth was a good fit with my new expectations; our hard work was making room for a variety of grape far better suited to the climate. I began thinking of row after row of shiraz, then bottle after bottle, then glass after glass – I was quite tipsy by the time I pulled out the last stake. But now, the prospect of making soap rekindles something. I have goosebumps.

Gianni comes up from the restaurant with left-overs from last night and some spicy sausage he made a few months ago. The chairs beside our beds are borrowed for extra seating, and we all gather around the table on the patio for our first family meal.

This is what WWOOFing is all about: sharing food and time, culture and ideas. These hours were our favourites at *Il Mulino*; the long unwind from a morning of activity.

Gianni pours wine into our glasses. We help ourselves to food. Riley declines the offer of risotto and starts nibbling on a slice of bread.

'You no like?' Gianni asks him.

He shakes his head.

'But you like pasta, yes?'

With a nod from Riley, Gianni disappears into the house and returns ten minutes later with a bowl of penne mixed with tomato sauce. Riley's smile meets his. Gianni is animated in his pleasure. Feeding people, I think, is what makes his life good.

We start to eat. I've been looking forward to relaxing with our hosts and getting to know them.

'Stromboli looks so close, is it possible to go there?' I ask.

Aidan's fork stops halfway to his mouth and doesn't resume until Gianni starts to answer.

'Yes, of course, it is only a few hours. But if you want to climb to the crater, you must stay overnight.' Gianni leans across the table and fills Riley's plate with more pasta. 'I have a friend with a boat who could take you.'

Aidan is bopping up and down on his chair asking what day we can go.

'I will talk to him and let you know,' says Gianni.

It doesn't take long for last night's leftovers to disappear into our appreciative stomachs and my glass to empty of wine. I pour another in anticipation of a long chat – we don't have to work again until it's time to wash up after dinner, and our afternoon has taken on the glorious dimensions of a long stretch of golden sand.

This is not, unfortunately, the reality for our hosts. Luca and Sophie are fighting, like small children do, and Lauren is distracted. It's reason enough to clear the table, and before it really starts, the conversation comes to an end.

~

Carluccia doesn't speak English, but her smile welcomes me into her kitchen and sits me at a large wooden table. There's a worn sofa facing a television and a couple of plain cabinets holding stuff of the everyday. There's nothing irrelevant or ornamental.

Carluccia and Lauren embrace, laughing at something the older woman has said as the words flow between them. The tension Lauren seemed to be holding in her shoulders before we walked through the door has loosened, and she moves with an easy grace around the kitchen, filling a pot with water, collecting bowls and forks and glasses, an onion and a knife. She touches Carluccia's arm and asks for something. Carluccia smiles at her daughter-in-law, then crosses to the storeroom on the other side of the hallway. She brings back pasta sauce and a bottle of wine.

By the time Carluccia has poured three glasses, the room has filled with the aroma of onion and garlic sizzling in olive oil. It never fails to make my mouth water. I sip the wine: it's rough, not made for celebrating but for nourishment. I love this about Italy – the ordinariness of wine, and of good food. I have another sip and consider the scene. I wouldn't find it in *Home Beautiful*, or a glossy tourist mag about Italy, but there's an essential beauty brought to it by these two women, the shared preparation of a meal, their warm affection for each other.

We eat. I smile a lot and use the few Italian words at my disposal to flatter the meal and Carluccia's hospitality. Then we go outside to make soap.

A large cauldron, blackened and beaten, sits above a fire pit in what I'm told is the old smoke-house. It's a small shed with broken shelves and rusted hooks, filled with bits of junk held together by cobwebs. When Carluccia lights the wood pile, we begin to choke. Smoke fills the small space, and Lauren and I move into the fresh air beyond the doors. Carluccia stays where she is, just inside the doorway, fanning the flames.

Water is the first ingredient. Lauren and I bring buckets, filled to the top, and Carluccia pours them into the cauldron. After that it all becomes a bit Shakespearian. Carluccia motions for us to start adding elderflowers. The delicate white clusters wilt and grey as they hit the surface of the water and, just as it's beginning to move with heat, Carluccia uses an enormous wooden ladle to push them under. All three of us lean over to watch.

Carluccia's neighbour joins us. He's brought a bucket of pigs' lard and a barrel of rancid olive oil. The old woman grabs great handfuls of the fat and adds it to the potion. She instructs her neighbour to pour in oil while she adds more wood to the fire. Flames lick the cauldron and smoke rises. She stirs, both hands holding the ladle, her whole body pushing it around. Cracked lips move, and I hear a murmured spell.

'She's trying to work out how much caustic soda to add,' says Lauren.

The murmuring stops. Boxes of caustic soda are dragged from a back corner of the smoke-house, they're damp, their contents clumping like old baking powder. Carluccia puts on rubber gloves and opens the first box. She empties it into the cauldron to combine with the fat and the flowers. Steam rises, and I wonder at the state of her lungs.

More flowers are needed. They seem out of place amongst the other ingredients, and I guess out loud that they might be for scent.

'No,' says Lauren. 'The flowers contain saponins, chemicals needed to make soap. She usually uses ivy, but the elderberry is in bloom, so she thought she'd try it.'

The blossoms go in, more lard, more rancid olive oil, more caustic soda. Carluccia stirs, never tiring. She utters more spells, this time calling for salt and ash. The ash has been sifted until it's as fine as flour. When she throws it into the cauldron it catches in the rising steam and a black cloak settles on her head and shoulders. The ladle moves around and around. The rest of us stand mute and transfixed.

The cauldron bubbles. The potion begins to thicken. Every now and then Carluccia scoops up a ladle-full and examines it. She is not yet satisfied.

'She wants it to become a bit glutinous before she lets the fire die,' Lauren tells me.

Hours after she started, Carluccia removes her gloves. She's seen a change in her concoction and scoops some out, holding it in the ladle for a minute to cool. A thick, work-worn finger dips into the tacky substance. She smears it on the back of her other hand, nods, then sets the ladle down.

The cauldron of soap will now be left overnight to cool and solidify, but Carluccia must do one more thing to ensure its success. From the basket of kindling used to feed the fire, two twigs are chosen, one placed across the other, and the symbol rested carefully on top of the soap. The spell is cast.

~

Lauren issues instructions each day, with priorities identified and tight timelines emphasised. She wants the fence around the chicken-run finished by the end of the week.

Large rolls of chicken wire lie around the perimeter of the area to be fenced. It's vast, about fifty metres square, with a scattering of fruit trees and a mesh of runner grass covering the surface. This grass is the reason for the fence. Like kikuyu – that hardy, drought-tolerant grass of the suburban Australian lawn – this Italian version creeps ever forward, its blind tendrils searching for purchase and strangling everything in its path. It's a food grower's nightmare: no barrier can contain it, no poison keeps it down. We feel at one with Lauren as she describes her fight with this horticultural foe. As a last stand she's decided to capture it, cage it, and hand it over to the chickens. It will take a long time, but Lauren thinks that eventually the grass will be beaten, the cage will be removed and food will grow. We'll be her mercenaries: Lauren gives her orders and leaves us to begin the battle.

Shannon swings the mattock and cracks the ground. I follow with the shovel and dig out the loosened clods of earth. It's a dense clay soil that sticks to our boots and makes them heavy.

We settle into a sustainable pace, begin to sweat, start talking about how we could use chickens to kill the kikuyu threatening our veggie patch at home. After only half an hour and four metres of trench, Lauren returns and tells us to down tools. We need to go to the *laboratorio* – Franco has decided to start bottling the wine.

The *laboratorio* is where fruit is preserved and wine is fermented, bottled and stored. It's large and modern, clean and organised. We're led through the preserving room to the wine room, where four shining vats stand tall in the centre. There's a long bench supporting a bottling machine, and shelves line the walls. Most are packed with empty green bottles placed so precisely that they're like infantry waiting to be deployed.

Franco is fiddling with the filtering machine.

'Hello, hello. You are welcome, come in.' He straightens up, his whole face smiling, large black-rimmed glasses falling down his nose. He pushes them up. 'We have a problem,' he says, though his smile indicates otherwise. 'The machine, it is not working. Maybe, Shannon, you can help me.'

Shannon tries, while I stand useless. 'Have you tried turning it off and on again?' I suggest. It seems to work with computers.

They look at me like I've just sneezed, then turn back to the machine. An hour passes. Gianni comes in and confidently tries everything that Franco has already tried. Then in a lightbulb moment (I can see it on his face) he turns the machine off.

My heart is beating as they stand silent for a minute or two, giving the machine time to consider its future. Then Gianni leans down and flicks the switch to turn it on again. Nothing happens.

'It was worth a try,' Shannon says, with a quick wink in my direction.

The three of them fiddle a bit more, then stand back and contemplate the mystery of the machine. I'm reminded of my baking day at *Il Mulino*, and of Stefan. Finally, Gianni does something with a wing nut, and wine from the closest vat flows through. There's much celebration, and Franco embraces Shannon. We're in business.

Four empty bottles are attached to the bottling machine, ready to receive the filtered wine. They begin to fill, and Franco tells us that the machine is designed to cut the flow when the wine is an inch from the top.

'This is the first year we have used this machine, last year it was much slower.'

The smile hasn't left his face, and it's contagious. Gianni shows me how to attach the bottle tops, stressing the importance of getting the angle right so that air doesn't get in and spoil the wine. Franco passes over the first full bottle, then the second. The third overflows, washing red over the bench and floor. Franco detaches the bottle and lifts the valve so the wine stops flowing.

'Not perfect.' He grins. 'We will watch that one.'

Confident in my technique, Gianni returns to the restaurant to prepare for dinner. Shannon takes over the bottling, and

Franco makes adjustments to the filtering machine. I'm nervous of spoiling the wine, and the bottles pile up.

'It's okay, take your time, you'll get used it.' Franco says.

It doesn't take long for our movements to become practised and automatic. We fall into step and begin talking. Franco is interested in what we think about farming and politics and people. His own thoughts bounce off ours. About Berlusconi, he's animated in his disdain and excited about the swing to the left in recent local elections – 'it might be portentous,' he says. About farming, he humbly bows to the seasons, makes tentative plans and expects them to change. About people, he repeats his last point. Franco thinks we are similar to plants.

'If we fail to thrive we should change the conditions we live in,' he says. But he admits that some people are like plants that have been grown indoors. 'Their stems are weak and they are easily bruised; achieving their potential growth is difficult.'

As he talks, I'm wondering if I'm one of those people who've spent too long indoors, been fed and watered too regularly.

When Lauren arrives, Franco and I are stacking a shelf with wine and singing 'Ten Green Bottles' – my contribution to our wide-ranging discussion. We've achieved less than she had hoped.

'I think the filter is slow, I don't know why,' says Franco in response to her concern.

Lauren suggests the job only needs two people, and when Franco leaves she dismisses Shannon back to the trenches. I'm sorry to see them go.

Lauren is frustrated by the filter. 'It will take days at this rate,' she says, surveying the set-up with her hands on her hips.

I imagine her schedule of tasks is being compromised. I'm no stranger to this state of mind, but I'm disappointed to find it here. When I think about it, my life has been all about productive efficiency ever since Aidan was born. He was five weeks old when I went back to work. It was just ten hours a week from home, but a lack of paid maternity leave made it necessary. I thought it would be easy to find ten hours in the week to focus on something other than a newborn … what an idiot. I couldn't manage breakfast let alone report writing. Whenever I sat down to either, Aidan demanded to be fed. One morning, Shannon noticed my cereal going soggy and started spoon-feeding me: two tasks got done at once. I calculated a time saving of about ten minutes that I could now allocate to the report. After that I became a bit obsessed with finding ways to save time (Weet-Bix on the loo was a breakthrough, but also an early sign that one day I'd need to see a psychologist).

Moving to the Adelaide Hills should have cured me of this work ethic – multi-tasking seemed incongruous with the slow lane we thought we'd changed into – but adding fruit trees and chickens to a four-day working week, a degree and the needs of small children seemed to intensify it. I never felt we were getting enough done, and out of habit I hurried everyone along.

I want to share this with Lauren, find out if her anxieties are similar to mine, tell her about Ulrike's daily repose. But she's in such a hurry that it doesn't feel like the right time.

~

After lunch, Lauren asks if we'd like a lift to the beach.

'We'd love a lift.' I'm acutely aware that our promise to the boys that we'd go swimming every afternoon has been well and truly broken.

'Do you mind taking Luca and Sophie with you?'

Neither Shan nor I answer immediately. I'm reviewing the image I had of the four of us walking along the shore, the boys picking up shells and interesting bits of driftwood.

'Of course not.' I say. To my ears, it's unconvincing.

'Could you make sure they put on sunscreen? Luca got quite burnt the other day. Have you got sunscreen?'

I nod.

From the farm, the ribbon of sand outlining the coast looks clean and unmarked by the feet of summer holiday makers. They'll arrive in droves, but not for another few weeks, and I've been looking forward to leaving the first prints on this stretch of beach. But when we arrive, it's hard to see the sand for the debris, and as Lauren drives off I regret that the children aren't wearing shoes.

'Be careful of all the glass, kids, and try not to step on anything rusty.'

It's warm, but the beach is deserted. Resorts snooze along the shoreline, waiting for the tourist season to start, oblivious to the rubbish and the drifts of grey, polluted sand. There's nowhere we want to lay our towels, but we choose a spot just in front of a sand hill littered with old tires and bits of timber. Luca and Sophie strip down to their underpants. They're brown and chubby: suntanned cherubs. Aidan and Riley are in broad-brimmed hats, long shorts and rashies with sleeves to their elbows. I can imagine what Franco would say if he saw them: 'Nothing will grow well without a good amount of sunshine.' Ah, for a Mediterranean complexion. I make my kids submit to sunscreen on all exposed skin, then call to Luca.

'Luca, come over here for a minute. Your mum wants me to put sunscreen on you.'

'No.'

'Come on. You'll get burnt if you don't.'

'No.'

'Well, you'll have to put your T-shirt back on if you don't want sunscreen.'

'No.'

I have to admit, I'm thrown. Luca is running circles around me, literally. He laughs each time he comes close, it's a kind of taunt. I want to reach out and grab his chubby arm, hold him still until his back is white with sunscreen, but I'm afraid to manhandle someone else's child. Shannon is no more successful, and when our store of mild threats and unconvincing bribes is exhausted (we only have apples and a few dry biscuits), we give up. Sophie is more pliant. She sits quietly in my lap and lets me rub the cream over her skin. With her finger she begins drawing in the sand.

The surf is rough, and there's a rip. None of the children are good swimmers, so we tell them not to go in. Aidan and Riley understand why and begin building a sand fort. Sophie is only interested in the patterns she's making. With these three, I can relax. But Luca wants to feel his heart beating. He's taken up the challenge of the sea and runs towards the waves, a little deeper each time. I have to call him back over and over. I feel myself frowning, and I resent it. This is more work than weeding or pulling stakes out of the ground.

Salvation comes from the mound of debris behind us. Aidan is looking for treasures and has decided to dig out one of the old tyres. Shannon is about to tell him to stay clear of the junk when the tyre comes rolling down the hill towards Luca.

'Look out, Luca,' Shannon calls.

Luca turns, and from that moment the waves lose their appeal. All three boys spend the next hour dragging tyres up the beach and rolling them down to the shore. Shannon supervises, while I draw starfish in the sand for Sophie. Any thoughts of tetanus are pushed, kicking and screaming, to the back of my mind.

Shadows stretch across the beach as black clouds move in from offshore. Fat drops of rain begin to fall. We abandon the tires, pack up the towels and hurry the children into T-shirts. I'm hoping Lauren has noticed the weather and is on her way to pick us up. We wait in the rain for ten minutes before she arrives.

'Have a good time?' she asks.

I lie and say yes, but I'm wondering if these hours of childcare will be counted towards our daily work quota. It's not a thought I would have had at *Il Mulino*, but I'm feeling miserly as I wait for Lauren to thank us for looking after her children.

'Aidan, your mum told me you like to cook. Would you like to help make the marmalade tomorrow?'

A kindness – now I don't know what to think.

~

We meet Lauren, and Franco's wife, Rosie, in the *laboratorio* at half past eight the next morning. Two stainless steel benches are set up at a right angle. There's a meat slicer and electric juicer on one, a chopping board and several large bowls on the other. Boxes of oranges are on the floor. We are each given a starched white apron and hair net.

Our tasks are decided: I'll wash the oranges, Lauren will cut them in half, Rosie will slice one half and pass the other to Aidan, whose job it will be to juice them. He is splendid in his whites; dimples accentuate his smile like speech marks – 'This is so great,' they say.

The process begins. Aidan retrieves his first half-orange, positions it on the tip of the juicer then flicks on the power. The motor screams. Aidan's dimples disappear in a frown of concentration, both hands pushing down on the orange to squeeze out every drop. When the bowl is full of juice, he pours it into the bucket with orange slices then returns to squeeze some more. It's a choreographed dance, the drone of the juicer setting our pace.

Then the acrid smell of burning. Lauren tells Aidan to stop, 'We'll have to let it cool for half an hour before we start again,' she says.

Aidan and I sit on old crates just outside the *laboratorio*.

'It looks like a shadow today,' Aidan says.

'What does?'

'Stromboli. Compared to when we arrived, it looks like a shadow.'

'It does, you're right. We're looking at it through the sea haze.'

'I can't even see the smoke.' He leans forward, as if it will help.

'Me neither. I think the longer I stare at it the less visible it becomes.'

'You should look away for a while. Then you'll be able to see it again.' He's right. And for a while we turn our heads from Stromboli to the beach, Stromboli to the beach.

'Can we go to Stromboli tomorrow?' he asks.

'I don't know, sweetheart. The haze might be a problem, but we'll ask Gianni.'

'If we can't go there, can we go to the beach?'

'Maybe,' I say.

'Without Luca and Sophie?' He says it quietly, into the flesh of my arm.

There's so much they don't say. Yesterday, at the beach, I thought it was just Shannon and me who felt the intrusion. But now, with his hand in mine and his cheek against my arm, Aidan is asking if he and Riley can have us all to themselves.

'Of course we'll go to the beach,' I say. 'But let's not wait till tomorrow. Let's go this afternoon. We could go to the little cove you saw when we got off the train. It's a bit of a hike, but that'll be part of the fun.' I won't break this promise. After all, we're free to do what we want.

'Thanks, Mum,' he says, wrapping both arms around me and squeezing tight.

Not for the first time, I wish we could afford to hire a car – it would make our freedom more convincing.

Soon the acrid smell has left through the open doors and the juicer is rested. Aidan takes his place, and our production line resumes. By one o'clock we have filled two large tubs with slices of fruit and juice. Rosie weighs them then measures out the sugar – about forty per cent of the weight of the fruit. She adds the sugar to the buckets and tells us they need to sit overnight.

'Tomorrow we will cook the fruit and put the marmalade in jars. You can come back and help with that if you like.'

When we arrive the next morning, Rosie is stirring the marmalade. Her long wooden spoon reminds me of Carluccia, but Rosie is no potion-maker. Her cauldron is an industrial double boiler, stainless steel with a temperature gauge and heavy, airtight lid. There's a release valve for steam and a ceiling exhaust to take it all away. I can't imagine pig fat or a vat of rancid olive oil being stored anywhere on these premises.

The marmalade has been cooking for about twenty minutes when Lauren smears a small amount onto a hand-held device called a refractometer.

'We have to put the sugar content on the labels. It also helps us decide how much pectin we need to use.'

She records the reading in an exercise book, then gets out a calculator and enters all the relevant numbers. The amount of pectin is decided, mixed with a little sugar and added to the boiler. Exactly three minutes later the boiler is turned off and we are put to work pouring the hot marmalade into sterilised jars. Thin crescents of orange are held in a glassy jelly.

Aidan has been attentive and diligent and useful. Before we leave the *laboratorio*, Lauren presents him with the last jar of marmalade, three-quarters full.

'Your own private jar,' she says. 'You don't have to share it with anyone.'

When we head to the beach Aidan's face is sticky with a marmalade smile. It takes an hour, but when we reach the little cove we're delighted. The beach is an undeveloped oasis embraced by craggy outcrops of black volcanic rock. Underfoot it's more sand than shell, and – except for us – it's deserted.

Shannon and I lay down towels and collapse onto them, wriggling to create the most comfortable contours. There will be no anxious watching. Between swims and snacks the boys build a fortress of sand and rock. They dare the calm sea to rise up and challenge them, but the sea is in no mood for combat. It retreats inch by inch, marking time along the shore, and the fortress grows ever larger.

~

'You need to work like a tractor.'

Lauren is telling us how to weed between the strawberries. Loosen, pull, loosen, pull. She'll be disappointed if we don't get through the patch by lunchtime. The trowel is driven into the ground. Soil rises, releases its hold. With deft fingers, Lauren pulls the weeds free and throws them in a pile.

'It's not that hard, but the last WWOOFers would take half a day to do a single row.'

She's told us this before. The last WWOOFers worked in slow motion, she doesn't want us to form the same habit.

I bite my lip, and take a deep breath – we're being performance managed. Despite this, I'm looking forward to the job. Lipstick-red, the strawberries are sweeter than any we've had back home. When the boys have written in their journals they'll join us.

The strawberry patch is hidden behind tall shrubs, and we're grateful for it when Lauren leaves.

'What kind of tractors should we be?' Shannon asks.

'Oh, I think you have the potential to be a mega horse-power John Deere, but I'm more like one of those rusty old farm relics that constantly needs to stop for a bit of mechanical tinkering.'

'Can I do the tinkering?'

'It'll slow you down.'

'That's why we're here isn't it?'

This is becoming a pattern. Lauren explains our task for the day, impresses upon us the need for speed, and then leaves us to wonder why she's in such a rush. Yesterday, it was the carrot seedlings. We needed to clear the beds of weeds, leaving only the carrot tops. It sounded easy, but then we saw the beds. The carrots were still tiny, and they shared the soil with thousands of juvenile weeds: same height, same colour, slightly different leaf – though you wouldn't know that unless you carried a magnifying glass and a heavy tome on botany. We hadn't packed either.

'If we don't get rid of the weeds, they'll smother the carrots,' she told us. 'It shouldn't take you too long.'

The tip of my nose brushed the ground as I examined the first weed. After half an hour I'd pulled out fifteen carrot seedlings along with approximately three hundred and seventeen weeds. When I got up to stretch my aching back, I looked along the length of the twenty-metre bed and realised I'd travelled no more than a metre.

Then I fell over.

I told Shannon it was from the shock, but in all honesty it was just the bending and stretching. Luckily I landed on my bum, but unluckily I landed on the carrots seedlings I'd just rescued.

'Wouldn't it make sense to let it all grow a bit taller and then weed around the seedlings?' I suggested to Shannon as he got me comfortable in the shade of a tree. 'These weeds have only been out of the ground for a day; there'll probably be three times as many next week.' If there's nothing I like more than innovative multi-tasking, there's nothing I like less than wasted effort.

'The good thing about WWOOFing, Pip, is that by the time the weeds we can't see have grown, we'll be gone.'

But I wasn't so sure. We had another two-and-a-half weeks – plenty of time to find ourselves sitting here again, remembering this conversation and feeling like we were nothing more than farm machinery, broken down and unreliable, perhaps, but farm machinery all the same.

Today, the boys find us sitting in the dirt eating strawberries as big as golf balls. I rub the flesh against my lips and pucker,

Shannon obliges, and the boys groan. We show them how to pull the weeds without dislodging the fruit. Riley reminds us that they're too young to be WWOOFers, so they tiptoe through the strawberry patch instead, picking the best of the crop.

'We should never have told them they didn't have to work,' I say to Shannon.

'Yeah, I wouldn't mind subcontracting every now and then.'

Aidan plonks himself at the end of a row, a half-eaten strawberry staining his hands. 'When will we go to Stromboli?' he asks.

'Gianni said the sea was too rough last week. His friend's boat needs calm weather to get there safely.' Shannon says it with an optimistic tone, but throws me a sceptical look. Every few days he has asked Gianni about going to Stromboli. Every few days there's been a reason it can't happen. 'Maybe this week will be okay,' he offers.

'Do you think it will explode while we're here?' Aidan asks.

'Maybe it will explode just as we're getting off the boat. Would you like that?' I ask.

'Yeah! That would be so cool.'

When the boys have had their fill and the rows are neat and weedless, we pack up our tools and buckets and head back to our room to clean up for lunch.

Whether by design or circumstance, we've been spending less and less time with Lauren and her family. We've not been invited back to lunch since that first day, so the restaurant is now our midday stomping ground. Today, like most days, the guests are all at the beach or exploring nearby towns, so we have the restaurant all to ourselves.

We've come to look forward to it. The fare is simple and good: white bread and provolone cheese, rough slices of prosciutto and, if we're lucky, leftovers from the night before. Without the protocol of dinner, it's less awkward. I know where the wine is, and Gianni has insisted I help myself. After we've eaten we can linger with the boys, help them with school work, listen to them fighting over the soccer table. We're not required to weed or wash up for anybody else, and we have none of our own domestic hooks to pull us away from doing nothing in particular together.

While I wait for the coffee to brew, I run my finger across the spines of books on the restaurant bookshelf. It's an eclectic collection, most likely Lauren's rejects and books left behind. I pick out an old tourist booklet about Tropea, a seaside town just ten minutes away by train:

> 'You will discover the echo of the people who lived here, in the fascinating explosion of colours and cosmic throbs enveloping the restless cliffs of the hills, the melodic rustling of the waves, the soft and pleasant caressing of the white sands and the bright roar that embraces you with its endless motion, that is the sea breeze.'

Who in their right mind wouldn't want to visit this magical place? 'Our next day trip,' I say to Shannon, placing the booklet in front of him.

'Of course,' he says, pushing our *Lonely Planet* guide across the table, open to the page describing Tropea as a puzzle of lanes and piazzas, with sunsets the colour of amethyst. I look for a reference to 'cosmic throbs', but find nothing.

~

Tropea's main street is decorated with tacky souvenirs, red onions and chillies. It's famous for all three, but the combination is a dizzying kaleidoscope of kitsch that is, I have to admit, making my head throb – though there's nothing 'cosmic' about it. We're caught in a swarm of day-trippers. The street hangs in front of us like flypaper, and one by one we're all becoming stuck to its colourful sides. Only the odd person escapes to venture down Tropea's meandering side streets and discover a more tranquil, and infinitely more beautiful, place.

Today, we are the ones who get away. The town wends this way and that, as if the streets were laid out by someone who'd just consumed a barrel of beer. We stop for lunch at a *trattoria*, empty despite being minutes from the main drag where people are waiting for tables at overpriced restaurants. We're seated near the front – their best table.

Pizza Margarita and fried whitebait, two beers, two lemonades. It's modest but feels celebratory; our first meal out for weeks. The waiter carries his two-year-old nephew on his hip as he takes our order. When he brings the obligatory basket of bread, the toddler crawls between his legs, forcing a little dance.

Our stomachs full, we take the meandering route from the restaurant to a once-grand staircase that leads down to the beach. It's dotted with bathers now, but in a few weeks it'll be blanketed with beach towels and burnt bodies as Europe takes its summer holiday. We walk along the shore and hand over ten euros for two beach chairs and an umbrella. We want to replicate our perfect day in Positano.

The sand here is more forgiving and far more beautiful than the volcanic grey of the Amalfi Coast. The boys begin digging another fort, but they're distracted by the broken tiles that freckle the shore. Each handful of sand is an excavation of treasure: they pick out beautiful fragments of colour, and Riley sorts them into piles on the end of my beach chair. There's a lot of white, but they're all subtly different. A paint catalogue would name them *clotted cream*, *snow cap*, *frosting*. The blues are more distinct; dark blue is rare and my favourite, sky blue dominates. Then there are the earthy colours, the browns and oranges that aren't very beautiful on their own, but together become the fallen leaves of an Adelaide Hills autumn. Suddenly we're all a little homesick. The tiny blue stones that look like lapis lazuli are actually, Shannon informs us, bits of coral, but we decide to keep them anyway.

'These red bits are coral as well,' he's saying to Aidan. He used to be a marine ecologist – it was his first big dream, and he made it come true. When his research funding ran out he got a job as a garbage collector.

'Do you miss it?' I ask.

'Miss what?'

'Spending your days on rock platforms collecting shells.'

'I only spent some of my days on rock platforms – most of the time I was in a lab, or crunching numbers at a computer.'

'But it's all you wanted to do as a kid, surely you miss it a bit.'

'I really don't. To be honest, I got more satisfaction out of being a garbo. Society would fall apart if bins weren't emptied – it puts counting molluscs at Botany Bay into perspective. And the hours were better.'

I watch him explain coral to the boys and wonder what kind of parent I'd have been if Shannon hadn't been around so much. A frustrated one, I suspect.

I join the boys in the sand and start sieving it through my fingers.

'Where do all the tiles come from?' Riley asks.

'Maybe they were washed into the sea after Vesuvius erupted. Maybe they're two thousand years old,' Aidan suggests.

'Maybe,' I say. 'Though I don't think this tile was ever part of a mosaic in Pompeii. See the grid pattern on the back? I think it was meant for a bathroom in one of those resorts.'

'We should throw those away,' Riley says, 'As well as the tiles with sharp edges. Let's just keep the ones from Pompeii.'

'What do you mean, *keep*?' I ask.

'We should take them home. You let Aidan take home rocks from Vesuvius, we should take these home as well.'

I can't argue because I've already started to imagine the mosaic we'll create together. 'I guess we could collect tiles instead of snow domes or tea towels, but you'll have to convince Dad. He's bound to end up carrying them.'

Dad thinks it's a terrible idea, but the sun and the beach chair have made his brain soft and he hasn't the ability to argue.

Sage advice from more than one person at the farm leads us to Tonino's gelateria on *Corso Vittorio Emanuele* – when we arrive, we're breathless from the walk up the hill. Tonino himself is behind the counter. We know it's him because of his likeness to a gilt-framed portrait of a laughing man with a hooked nose and friar's bald patch that hangs on the wall above him. The wrinkles around his eyes as he greets the boys are identical, though his hair is greyer. Behind him, a machine is churning his latest invention. Tonino makes his own gelato, which, I was devastated to find out, is not the case for most gelaterias. We have come to taste his famous red onion gelato, but it is not the only flavour that intrigues us.

Red onion is very oniony, but surprisingly sweet. We're not as taken with cactus or salami, but the fig goes down very well and a few favourites set the bar high for future gelato eating. Tonino chats to us in Italian as if we understand what he's saying. We understand a little, and with new-found confidence I venture to ask, in Italian, if he makes Pokémon flavour. He looks bewildered.

Back at the farm we contemplate our pile of coloured tiles. We guess a kilo – too much to carry around for another couple of months. No one except Shannon wants to leave the tiles behind, so we decide to post them home along with our woollens, a couple of much-loved books and Aidan's rocks from Vesuvius.

It marks a transition, a shedding of skins – into the box go all of the things we thought we might need but didn't and all of the things we once needed, but don't any more. We realise that we're halfway through our journey.

'Only halfway?' Aidan moans. 'It feels like we've been away forever.'

'Are you homesick?' I ask, although I'm not sure I know what to do with the answer.

'Kinda. I miss my room.'

'What about you, Riley, are you homesick?'

'Um, not really, but do we have to stay here much longer?'

'Another week and a bit. Can you last that long?'

'Yeah, maybe.' His voice is small and he's looking at the floor.

Looking at Riley now, I wonder if we're expecting too much from them, leaving them alone for hours at a time in unfamiliar places, with people they barely know and sometimes don't get on with. The other day, after a morning digging trenches for chicken fencing, Shannon and I found Riley cocooned in his bed. He was tired, he said, but Aidan told us later that Luca had picked up Riley's DS and threatened to throw it on the ground if they didn't play with him. I imagine what that meant to Riley. His DS is the only constant in his life right now. When he feels lonely or homesick, when the strangeness of a place overwhelms him, it gives Riley a place to retreat to. Aidan told me Riley froze, that tears welled in his eyes as Luca held the DS above his head. Hours later I sat on the bed and stroked his hair. I explained that Luca is only six and doesn't realise the importance of things. It was no consolation. Riley is only nine: the importance of things weighs heavily. I realised then, later than I should have, that the DS comes a distant second to Shannon and me.

Now, with his head bowed, and his small voice telling us he's not happy here, we consider our options. If we want, we could leave tomorrow. If we had a car, we could leave today. We talk about it, but Shannon and I lack the impulsiveness of the true intrepid traveller – and we lack the cash. If we left now we'd have to pay for ten days' food and accommodation that we didn't anticipate. We decide to stick to the plan, but to be more assertive. One of us needs to always be available to the boys. That means we work nearby or they come with us, and at night, one of us will always come back to our room with them, no matter how much washing up there is.

It feels like the kind of discussion working parents have all the time – how to be there for your children and still earn a living. But it's a bit hard to believe we're having it here, in the south of Italy, where we have a view of an active volcano.

~

Steam is rising from the kettle on Lauren's stove. Her hand hovers, waiting for the whistle to blow before she takes it from the heat to fill the pot. I reach into the cupboard and pull out two mugs, conscious that this might be the last time.

This farm is potentially a WWOOFing heaven – the food, the view, even the hours – but after four weeks it's lost its shine. I've decided it's like a beautiful pair of shoes that give you blisters. I thought that by now Lauren and I would know each other and be comfortable, but her attention is always elsewhere. Today it reminds me of my own distraction. When the needs of work and home and children collide and ring noisily in my head, it's hard to hear Riley's small voice, or make room for details about Aidan's monsters. I often just nod and smile to give the impression that I'm listening. Lauren is nodding and smiling at me now – her response to my mundane enquiry about her morning. I realise, sheepishly, that this is no holiday for her.

I like to think I'd be different. I remember Stefan saying that every WWOOFer brought something of value to their farm, and that he just had to be observant and take time to listen to their story. But time, for them, was languid. I began walking slowly at *Il Mulino*, and I found I was never out of breath and never late. Since arriving at *Pirapora*, my pace has quickened, and I resent it. I want so much to be free from the tyranny of time and banish words like 'quick' and 'hurry'. I've been brought up to revere the clock. Lauren, I realise, is a daughter of the same congregation, though it doesn't suit the clothes she wears. On reflection, it doesn't suit mine.

I'm curious about what it is that distracts her, about what brought her here, and what makes her stay. I want to know what she thinks of this life and whether it's worth pursuing. But our conversations have been guarded, and I've had to rely heavily on observation. I've observed an efficient, frustrated, time-poor woman who quite possibly would prefer to be doing something else.

Tea is an opportunity to talk. Every few days, around eleven in the morning, she's boiled the kettle and put three heaped spoons of Twining's Earl Grey into a blue teapot. This releases my inquisitive tongue and allows Lauren to relax, just a little. We both understand the value of a good cup of tea in a country that venerates coffee. It's something else we have in common.

This time, she tells me that she attended Cambridge: 'Elitist and overrated, I couldn't stand it so I left.'

She never finished her degree, but she wants me to know this about her. She wants me to know that she's chosen this farming life from all the possible lives available to her. In addition to her native English, Lauren speaks Italian and German. Her bookshelves bow under the weight of knowledge. Philosophers and Booker Prize-winners cohabit with experts on permaculture and organic gardening. I can't help thinking her presence on this family farm is accidental. That what might have been just another experience has somehow snared her. Love will do that, and she fell in love with a man who dreamt of cooking home-grown organic food within clear sight of a volcano. It would have been easy to follow that dream, to tweak it and make it her own. But I want to know what it's really like, if she still loves it, what she would do differently. And I want to know what else she dreams of in the quiet moments of her life.

While my words struggle to compose themselves, she rinses her cup and pulls on her boots.

'How's the chicken fence going?' she asks.

'Great, it should be finished this afternoon.'

'Good, leave Shannon to finish it off, I want you to paint the new chicken house then help Rosie with the strawberry jam.'

I wash my cup and follow her out the door. A mouthful of questions dissipates on my tongue.

~

The chicken fence is magnificent. In a symbolic gesture of solidarity, the boys and I have rushed from the *laboratorio*, where we've been helping Rosie make strawberry jam, to assist Shannon in rolling out the final few metres of chicken wire. We've secured it to the last post, and it's fabulous. The chicken house, on the other hand, looks like it's been shat on by a flock of seagulls. The paint was a watery lime wash that had to be slapped on with a drenched brush. I was in a hurry to collect the boys so they could help with the jam, and I took less care than I should have.

From where we stand we can see the results of much of our labour over the past few weeks. Besides the fence and the chicken house there are tomato frames standing tall and straight, with newly pruned tomato plants tied neatly to the first row of bamboo and only a few grass twines unravelling from incompetent twisting. I'm pleased to see that several rows of carrots have survived my ministrations, though a new wave of weeds is beginning to push up the soil around them.

'Great job, Shan, you've ticked all the boxes on Lauren's list.'

'*We* have, you mean.'

He's being kind. It's becoming apparent that I'm not a natural in the field. Bending over to pull out weeds makes me a bit woozy. If I didn't take regular breaks I'd be falling all over the place. Shannon is quite happy to make up for my malingering, and without a word of reproof. Now, as he joins us under a shady tree, dirt sticking to his sweaty brow, we talk about what a good life we would have back home if we could replace paid work with digging and planting and harvesting food. It's a familiar conversation, but I'm staring at row upon row of seedlings in cracked earth, sticky with clay, and for the first time I notice how fragile they look. I change the subject.

'Here comes Franco,' I say. We stand to greet him. He's always smiling, his arms spread wide as if he's waiting for a hug.

'Wonderful, wonderful.' He's looking over at the chicken enclosure. 'Tomorrow we will move the chickens. It will be a celebration.' He turns to us and pats Shannon on the shoulder. 'We are so happy, you have done a wonderful job, thank you.'

His thanks is the first we've had in weeks. It's a mean thought, and I shake my head to dismiss it, reminding myself that our labour is paid for in risotto and tiramisu.

~

Franco arranges us like a guard of honour either side of an imagined path from the old chicken yard to the new.

'This won't work,' Shannon whispers to me.

We each have a length of bamboo which will be used, we are told, to herd the birds towards their new home. It's not far, perhaps ten metres, but our presence is likely to make the chickens suspicious. A crowd has gathered – Gianni has invited the guests, thinking it might be nice for them to see a working farm in action. Half of them insist on helping and more bamboo is handed around.

'A bucket of scraps and someone familiar would probably do the job,' Shannon says to me, as Rosie opens the gate of the old yard and starts to shoo out the chickens. They're reluctant. There are about twenty of them, not including the clucky hen and her brood of chicks – she's hiding them in a tangle of bushes and avoiding the evacuation.

The first hen out the gate is startled, perhaps by the warrior stance of Gianni to its left, and so it darts right. Lauren tries to corral it with her bamboo, shouting for others to back her up. I try to cut the frightened bird off before it runs into a row of carrots, but it keeps changing direction and I'm afraid of hurting it with the stick. More hens run out ahead of Rosie's flailing arms. The boys are delighted at the opportunity to brandish their spears and swords – the chickens are hordes of goblins emerging from a dark forest in Middle Earth.

Shannon isn't really moving. He stands near the entrance to the new yard with his bamboo horizontal and a smile that only I notice. The hens have scattered in every direction, and so have the people. Gianni and Franco are shouting instructions in Italian, German, English. I know Shannon is probably right and that this is a wild goose chase (or chicken chase), but the excitement is so infectious that I call to Aidan and Riley to go after a couple of hens that have darted their way.

After half an hour we've managed to usher one chicken into the new enclosure. It calls to the others, but they've disappeared. We're not sure that they'll even return to their original home.

Mumbled concerns about foxes and mild accusations of poor planning are heard above the clucking of the lonely captive. Franco dismisses the fox threat and decides to try again tomorrow, perhaps just him and a bucket of food. It occurs to me that Franco would find a kindred spirit in Stefan. It's not important to him that our efforts today didn't succeed. We will succeed tomorrow, or the next day. Together they would walk from here talking of something else, the chickens forgotten because thinking of them now is not productive. Gianni, Lauren and Rosie look defeated, but the rest of us peel away from the battleground in high spirits. It's the most fun we've had all month.

~

I'm alone in our room, and Lauren is moving about next door. *I won't miss her*, I write in my notebook, but before the thought unfurls I'm distracted by the first deep breaths of an accordion.

I recognise the tune from the soundtrack of *Amélie*, and smile at the memory of a little girl trying to make her finger 'pop' out of her mouth. Yann Tiersen's haunting melody slips into me like opium smoke. It loosens my mind and I begin to think differently about Lauren.

This is a quiet moment, all her own; one of the few in her busy life. Instead of resting or reading or watching television, she's making music. We've been here nearly a month and it's the first time I've heard her play. She plays beautifully. But she's not yet familiar with the piece. The conversation she's having with the music flows for a while, and then hesitates. Certain phrases repeat themselves, tentative, as though she's trying to work out their meaning. When she's sure, the conversation resumes and her expression is forceful, emotional.

I feel uncomfortable. Lauren has come across as so assured, even arrogant, in the way she lives this life. But now I wonder if it's some kind of armour she wears against subversive thoughts.

There's something I recognise, and am only beginning to understand. Over the past week or so I've lain awake long after Shannon and the boys have nodded off, a quiet truth nagging me as I drift between consciousness and sleep, a confession on the tip of my tongue that disappears before I know what it is. As I lie here now, listening to Lauren struggle with the melody, I begin to articulate it.

I thought I knew what we were looking for in Italy, that we'd recognise it and claim it and take it home in our backpacks to live happily ever after in the Adelaide Hills. But the closer I come to the life I think I want, the less familiar it is. I know what I've been hoping for – some kind of Eden – and together, Shannon and I have defined it. When we talk about it, we talk about planting and harvesting and bottling and going to market. We paint a picture of ourselves working together in the orchard or the kitchen, our downtime a shared meal with friends after turning a bumper crop of tomatoes into passata. But something has been left out.

When I'm alone with this dream of ours I think less about digging and more about making. Bread is where *our* dream and *mine* sit so comfortably together, but the truth that nags me might lie between the kneading and the baking, in those quiet hours when magic happens, when the dough rises of its own accord and my ideas have time to form. I know they're there; they whisper to me before I go to sleep, when I'm stuck in traffic, when I should be paying attention to the presentation of a colleague. But the only time I nurture them is while the bread grows, while it bakes, while it cools on the wire rack and fills the house with its promise. Before I've even finished kneading, words are being arranged into phrases, rehearsed and edited within the rhythm of movement that makes the dough elastic. As soon as I've washed the flour from my hands I start to write. By the time the dough has doubled in size I've written pages of words: fervent, crazy, soppy words; misspelt and shameful; honest and bare; stupid, senseless, experimental words that can be anything because they will be nothing. They dwell only in these quiet moments, and no one will ever read them. I've always thought that was enough.

I'm worried that I might lose something precious if I stay here listening to Lauren's lament for much longer, but my face is wet and my eyes swollen. I can't leave. The more I think about her, the more I feel a mirror is being held up for me to peer into, that some possible future is being foretold. It's not one I want to run to.

She plays her last note. She's been interrupted, so it hangs in the air, expectant, and we're both left with the unfinished song playing over in our heads.

~

Lauren is leaving today – a trip home to England. Her last instruction to us is to weed the garden bed that borders the footpath down to the restaurant. The boys are helping, and we're taking it easy, talking about our own departure – it feels long overdue.

'Does that mean we won't get to go to Stromboli?' Aidan asks. Since it disappeared behind the summer haze, we thought he'd forgotten about the volcano. We almost had.

'I'm afraid it does, mate,' Shannon says.

'It's not going anywhere,' I say. 'Maybe you'll come back and climb it when you're older.'

'Maybe,' he says, and I wonder if this will be a dream he carries with him, or if it will be put aside.

Gianni starts up the van not far from where we're digging. We turn to see Lauren bringing her bags from the house. She's animated and excited, smiling more than I've seen her smile since we got here. She sees us, gives the bags to Gianni and runs over.

'It was good to meet you, enjoy the rest of your trip.'

No more, or less, than that. We watch her skip back towards the van and I feel happy for her. I don't really care anymore that we're an afterthought – why should we be more than that? Just because she's part of our journey, doesn't mean we have to be part of hers. Before she gets to the van she turns, and, walking backwards, waves her hand.

'Thanks for all your great work,' she says. 'It's made a huge difference.'

Matera

(Be grateful)

Like all great escapes, ours begins under the cover of darkness, with whispered entreaties to hurry up and many misunderstood hand signals. I imagine us as runaways, fleeing a life of forced labour. Of course, our voluntary servitude on a Calabrian *agriturismo* is hardly comparable to a chain gang or the Gulag, but Lauren's directive to 'work like a tractor' did sound like a whip at our backs, and we *were* technically fed leftovers – though, just thinking of Gianni's leftover strawberry gelato is making my mouth water.

As everyone knows, a successful escape from toil requires three things: food, transport and a safe house. So in the early hours of the morning I sneak down to the farm restaurant for bread and cheese and a jar of Rosie's delicious strawberry jam. We have a long journey ahead, and we don't want to go hungry.

Our choice of transport requires a suspension of my imprisonment fantasy, as the success of our great escape relies heavily on a lift to the station from one of our captors. I almost have to abandon the fantasy altogether when Gianni buys us espresso and pastries at the station bar and wishes us a warm farewell. Custard drips down my chin, and I recall his generous portions of tiramisu and last night's gastronomic revelation: chocolate and orange-marmalade pizza. I feel a little guilty about casting him in the role of oppressor. After a kiss on both cheeks, I decide he's our man on the inside.

Three trains get us to the town of Sibari, where we lean against a low wall to wait for the bus that will take us to our safe house.

We watch as several men and a woman wearing a loose headscarf hang around a drinking fountain. The woman is brushing her teeth. A young man, when his turn comes, removes his shirt and splashes his torso with the cool clean water falling in a piddling arc from the spout. It takes a long while for him to collect enough to douse his dusty hair. Containers, large and small, are waiting to be filled. An older man comes from across the road with a shopping trolley containing two empty plastic drums. He hunches over it, leaning his thin chest on the handle bar, stretching his arms along the sides and holding the body of the cage, like a weary shopper. One wheel is fluttering uncontrollably. He joins the queue.

Some of the younger men are talking, in Arabic I think, though I'm guessing. The woman is silent. She takes her scarf off and brushes her long black hair. I wonder if she wishes for a mirror, or if vanity has been left behind with so much else.

'What are they doing, Mum?' Riley whispers in my ear. He's confused at seeing such private activities in a public place.

'I think they're refugees, darling. They've come to Italy for a better life, but there's no plumbing wherever they're living, so this is where they wash and collect water for drinking and cooking.'

'Why can't they live in a proper house?'

I can't think of a single good reason, so I pull him close and squeeze him as tight as I can without hurting him. He doesn't ask any more.

It reminds me that I've been playing at make-believe from a place of privilege and good fortune – our whole journey is only possible because of the life we take for granted. We're grateful when the bus comes. I take a last subtle look at the people queuing for the drinking fountain. They seem not to have noticed us at all, though perhaps it's only by pretending others aren't there that you can take care of personal hygiene in public. At this moment I'm not sure what would be kinder – to pay attention, or to turn away. What, after all, will we achieve by passively observing? I notice Riley watching them as he walks towards the bus, his brow is furrowed. Observation, I think, might achieve something – time will tell.

~

Matera has been carved out of a canyon and is thought to be one of the oldest towns on earth. Depending on which guidebook you read, it's been continuously inhabited for between five and nine thousand years. It's an intriguing stopover between Zambrone and Tuscany, and we've organised to spend one night in the *Sassi*, Matera's cave-dwelling district. We're all eager to lay eyes on them, but right now I'm not sure we'll make it before nightfall. We've walked through the same stone tunnel three times, and Shannon and I are having one of those arguments where we try to establish blame in the hope that, once that's determined, the way forward will magically be revealed.

I have a poor track record when it comes to reading maps, and the guidebook is presently in my hands. If I wasn't so tired and hungry I'd probably just hand the book to Shannon, apologise for the half hour of unnecessary hiking and let him take the lead. It takes a child to bring reason to my weary brain.

'I'm not going down there again,' says Aidan as we look through the now familiar tunnel. He plonks himself on the ground and refuses to move. 'Come and get me when you've found the hotel.'

It's not a bad idea, but Shannon decides instead to grab the guidebook from my hands and examine it himself. I watch his eyes move from the street sign to the map, and just as I'm about to say something sarcastic, he turns the map around and faces away from the tunnel. Is it possible I was holding it upside down? I decide to stay quiet, and when he leads off in a different direction, I gently encourage the boys to follow – though they now seem more willing.

Hotel Caveoso is, as the name implies, a series of caves. They've been tamed by stone extensions, neat archways and staircases, but when we enter the small lobby the temperature drops, sound is silenced, and there's a faint smell of limestone.

Our room is a bit of a shock, and the first thing I do is check the email we were sent confirming the modest price. It's beautiful and enormous. The bathroom is cavernous, literally. Behind a circular wooden door set into a stone archway we find two single beds – like the bathroom, this room is part of an original cave dwelling, and it doesn't take much to imagine a hobbit living here. We leave the boys to argue over who should be Bilbo and who Frodo and which bed each Halfling should occupy, and we step out onto the balcony to look at the view of *Santa Maria d'Idris*, a 900-year-old church carved into an imposing limestone cliff known as Monterrone.

'Time to explore,' I say to Shannon.

'Do you want to inform the boys or shall I?' he says.

They're sprawled across our bed, their eyes wide and unblinking, staring at the cartoon colour coming from the television.

~

If someone were leaning on a wall looking down on *Via Brunno Buozzi*, they'd see four strolling figures in no hurry for anything. The adults are joined at the fingertips, and the children move back and forth between them and things imagined, as if secured by a length of elastic. They look happy.

'I'm happy,' I say, to whoever might hear me.

'Why wouldn't you be?' Shannon replies.

'No reason at all, but I've just realised that the trick to happiness is recognising it, and I just did, so I thought I'd mention it.'

'Is it the little shampoos and conditioners, or the wide-screen TV?'

'It's the bidet, if you must know. But mostly it's the fact we're free to do as we like and choose what we eat, and at the end of the day we can put the boys to bed and close the door between their room and ours – it's exhilarating!' Shannon pulls me in a little closer.

The stairs don't seem so steep now. We follow them up and down, into quiet corners that end with old wooden doors we dare not open. Past old caves that haven't yet been gentrified, their dank interiors filled with rubbish and broken furniture. We're lost, but the *Sassi* don't go on forever and eventually paving stones give way to rough rock that falls away into the ravine. We sit down to get our bearings.

The sky seems close and enormous. Dark cloud glides under a silver blanket, animating the other side of the ravine with shadow and light. It's riddled with caves. They're prehistoric, abandoned lifetimes ago, and the people who sheltered in them are almost beyond my imagination. What I can guess is that they lived a hard and bleak existence.

I turn away and look back towards the *Sassi*, honeycombed in the late afternoon light. It's a monochrome landscape of stone and terracotta tiles underlined by a splash of red and blue and orange – clothes hung to dry between two buildings.

'I'm hungry,' Riley says.

Suddenly we're all aware of our grumbling tummies. We pass under the line of washing and return to the labyrinth.

When it comes to eating out I'm a bit neurotic. It happens so rarely that I want it to be just right. From Rome to Tropea I've dragged the family from menu to menu looking for the perfect meal. It's time-consuming and ultimately disappointing, and by the time we sit to eat, we're so hungry we'd be satisfied with a bowl of stale bread and yesterday's pizza. I have no urge to do that now. I feel that Matera, somehow, has taken us in hand and will deliver us to where we want to go. The pursuit of the perfect meal is probably a fool's errand anyway.

We wash up at *La Talpa*. We haven't booked but we're early, and there's a table for four tucked into a corner of the main cave. We splurge. I ask for pasta with fungi, rocket and truffle.

'Oh my God!' I've just had my first taste. 'This is what I was hoping for when I bought that truffle in Arezzo. What have they done that I didn't?'

'Hired a chef, I suspect,' says Shannon, quickly leaning over to kiss away my objection. 'And it's possible their truffle hasn't spent weeks in the bottom of a backpack with a bag of dirty undies,' he adds for good measure.

My love of truffle is restored. I pick up my wine glass and clink it against Shannon's beer and the boys' cans of Fanta.

We emerge from the cave, Shannon carrying a box of leftover pizza. The streets are dimly lit, beautiful and surreal, the air is still warm.

'Let's walk back the long way,' I suggest.

'Only if we can get gelato,' says Aidan.

There's not much left of the boys' gelato when we stumble upon a jazz quartet in *Piazza Sedile*. They're playing the kind of jazz that I love and Shannon is warming to. The sounds are smooth, and I'm quickly falling for the man playing the trumpet. Adam Rapa is bald, a little thick around the waist and the voice of his trumpet is like silky Italian hot chocolate. I start dancing. Music has a way of overriding my natural reserve, but it's too much for the boys, and Shannon has decided to sit this one out on the steps of an old palace. After five minutes Riley decides to burst my bubble.

'Mum, you look really weird, can you stop?'

'I'm enjoying the music, sweetheart.'

'But it's really embarrassing, and we want to go home'

It's these moments that start me thinking about life without the pull of family. I keep picturing myself alone in these cities and towns. Usually I'm younger, so perhaps it's just reminiscing (or wishful thinking), but sometimes I'm my 43-year-old self. Instead of working on farms I imagine I've rented a beautiful apartment with tall windows that let morning light fall across an old wooden desk. Tonight I will fall in love, and tomorrow I will spend all morning writing about it.

But Adam Rapa hasn't once looked in my direction. If Shannon and the boys weren't here I would, perhaps, dance a little longer, but when the trumpet finally stopped playing I'd have to wander back to that beautiful apartment alone. The joy of the moment might end up in a notebook, but it would remain unshared and be a prelude to nothing.

I look towards Shannon; he hasn't been completely indifferent to the sway of my body.

'Dance as long as you like,' he says, with a smile. But the boys just groan.

I relent, 'Okay, let's go,' I say. Riley takes my hand and we dawdle back to our room.

~

At breakfast, we're shown to a table laid for four in a little cave at the back of the dining room. It feels odd being a guest rather than a worker. I feel like a fraud and say 'thank you' too often.

I look at my hands, dry and scarred from all the work they've done since arriving in Italy. I'm proud of them, but I'm also glad to be able to give them some time off. I catch the eye of the waiter and ask him to bring me another coffee. We have this one day to be tourists before the work starts again.

Matera is a mixture of tamed and untamed rock. The church of *Santa Maria d'Idris* hasn't tried to discipline the caves in the way Hotel Caveoso has. Outside, the paving undulates over natural contours, moves around rocky eruptions, reaches under the ledge of a huge boulder. The boys run up and down the irregular slopes like surfers on the swell, then come to rest under the boulder, and it's as if a monster wave has frozen in time – I take a photo before it comes crashing down.

'Do you think that's the way in?' asks Aidan, pointing to a small doorway cut into a formidable lump of rock rising out of the ravine.

Its face is bright under a rising sun, but the sky above is troubled, dark grey and churning. It could be a dragon's lair. They hurry us up the stairs. When we approach the door we know we're entering something far more ancient than a 900-year-old church.

There's treasure aplenty, though not what any of us expected. A tunnel joins a large anteroom to an older series of caves. The floor is coloured flagstone, and the walls are fading frescos, some whole, others just fragments, sometimes no more than the rich hem of a saintly gown. The frescos were painted between the 12th and 17th centuries. Some have been restored, and their colours are almost garish. Most, though, look like memories lost in dementia.

I stare at them for a long time, trying to conjure the past. The caves of Matera were once full of people living in abject poverty. This church must have seemed like a haven, if not heaven itself. In my mind, the reverent whispering of tourists becomes the clamour of neighbours gossiping and solving problems, reigniting old arguments and insults. A priest enters and they all quiet down, some to listen, desperate to hear of an afterlife, and others just content to rest their tired bodies and settle their eyes on the beauty of the painted walls.

After we've lunched on cold pizza we make our way to *Casa-Grotta di Vico Solitario,* one of Matera's original cave dwellings. In the 1950s it became clear that living in a cave the size of a double garage with a few chickens, a pig, a donkey and six or seven siblings was bad for your health. A 50 per cent child mortality rate prompted the government to forcibly relocate the entire cave-dwelling population to concrete apartments on the less spectacular side of town. With the poor out of the way, proper sewerage and electricity could be installed, and all those uninhabitable caves were renovated to become hotels and restaurants, artisan studios and expensive homes.

Casa-Grotta has been preserved for the sake of history and the tourist dollar, but I suspect it's far more charming now than it might have been in the 1950s. Twenty tourists, at least, are squashed in here with us, so it's easy to imagine the feeling of claustrophobia. I hold tight to Riley's hand and pull him through spaces that barely exist. We look under the small bed and find four stuffed hens in a nesting box. In one corner of the room are a model donkey and pig. A small alcove just beyond is where food and hay and water were stored. The walls are hung with implements for cooking and cleaning and caring for animals. Close to where the family prepared food is what looks like a pit toilet – that would explain the 50 per cent child mortality rate. But no, it turns out to be a cistern, a typical feature of cave houses all over Matera. With no natural reservoirs, people needed to collect rainwater, and so the town is riddled with drains that funnel water into stone catchments carved out of the bedrock and accessed from within the caves. I'm reassured, though conscious, now, of a lack of toilet facilities.

A bassinette is set up by the bed, and there's a black-and-white photograph of a woman sitting on a wooden chair with a baby in her arms. Five other children press close around her. The dresser in the background is still here. The mother is smiling. By all accounts, six children, well-fed and healthy looking, was something to be happy about. I suspect she had little time for day-dreaming, but if she did, where would those dreams have taken her? What would a good life have looked like to her? Beyond the survival of her children, perhaps it resembled a neat and tidy apartment with indoor plumbing.

'I wouldn't like to live here,' says Riley.

'Why not?'

'It's way too crowded.'

'It sure is, especially today.'

'And there's nowhere to play soccer.'

The boys are used to space, so the crowds of cities have sometimes unnerved them. But I'm the product of a hive. It was nothing like the honeycombed squalor of Matera's 1950s *Sassi*, but as I imagine the life this family was moved to, I'm back in my childhood bedroom in an eight-storey apartment block in a crowded seaside suburb of Sydney.

As a child I spent endless hours imagining the lives lived on the other side of my bedroom wall. When I found it hard to sleep, I would piece together sound clues: the faint strains of music abruptly stopped, the slam of a door, then the central lift being summoned. It worked like an iron lung, that lift, bringing life in and out of our building, its mechanical hum regular and strangely reassuring. In fact, thinking of it now, I realise that I've always loved the closeness of strangers, that I find comfort in the way we buzz around each other – contact a constant possibility but never a requirement. It's easy to observe life in a city, and not be observed doing it. I think that's why I feel so comfortable in Matera. Why I love to sit in cafes. Why I enjoy travelling by train. And why, when I flew the nest that first time, it was a city I landed in.

We spend our last Matera hour in *Piazza Vittorio Veneto*, eating gelato and watching a wedding party have their pictures taken. The bride and groom wear white and florescent green. The sash around her waist matches perfectly with his sneakers, though it doesn't light up like his shoes do every time he takes a step – a small mercy.

The *Sassi* have disappeared behind the piazza. Matera, from this angle, looks no different to any other Italian town. Churches and noble homes mark the perimeter of a wide expanse of precisely cut paving stone. In the centre there's a fountain. It's all beautiful, and it's easy to watch the spectacle of the newlyweds, but it doesn't excite me like the *Sassi* do. I think I even resent it a little for turning its back on the cave dwellings and trying to be beautifully ordinary when it could have been something far more interesting.

I'm already missing this place, wishing we had more days to get to know it. We take a turn around the piazza, a farewell tour, and discover, behind the fountain, the ruins of an older Matera. The whole piazza sits on the roof of a Byzantine town, which included churches and a castle and houses for rich and poor. Looking down into one of the excavation pits, I'm reminded that history, and life, is a series of cover-ups and reinventions – each re-creation aiming to be better than the last. I have no idea if the lives lived above this ruin are better than the lives that were lived within it. Their expectations would have been different, but would joy and sadness have felt the same? I've felt joy in Matera, and I'm sad to leave so soon, but the real source of my joy will leave with me. I wrap an arm around each of the boys and pull them close, kissing each on the head in turn. Behind my back their arms intertwine, a rare gesture of brotherly affection.

Then a tussle begins. They pull and shove and start calling each other names. They ignore me when I ask them to stop – in my blissful state I've used an ineffective sing-song voice – so eventually I just push them away, and hiss.

The joys of motherhood can be so infuriatingly fleeting. Real joy, I suddenly think, would be sending Shannon ahead with these quarrelling boys and staying another night in Matera, alone. I had a dream last night that I wouldn't mind pursuing, it involved a bald man and a trumpet, and I danced until dawn.

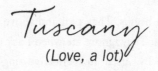

Tuscany
(Love, a lot)

Stefan gets out of the familiar white van and takes Shannon's right hand, holds his upper arm affectionately then pulls him into an embrace. Seconds could have passed, but it's been six weeks, and feels like months. We're back where we started.

The road into the Tuscan hills is familiar, and our journey to the farm is filled with conversation. Shannon sits in the front this time, he and Stefan are old friends with matching smiles, both faces weathered by outdoor lives. In the back seat I can watch them unnoticed. They're both precious to me, and I wonder if what I feel for Stefan is love, and if it is, what kind.

The van bumps along the dirt road leading to the house. It's like coming home.

'There's Amalie,' Riley says. She's steadier on her feet than when we last saw her. One small arm is raised in greeting, and she's bobbing up and down. Ulrike and Simona are there too, Marta is on the swing – they're all waiting for us.

A group of Germans have rented both apartments for a few weeks. Simona and Amalie have moved into the woodhouse, so we're given the room above the toolshed. It's tiny, much smaller than the woodhouse, but in my homecoming mood I see no discomforts, though I do note the deadly staircase – more of a ladder, really. I suggest to Shannon an alternative night-time toilet arrangement consisting of a bucket and excellent aim. Finding enough floor space for the bucket isn't easy, but we squeeze it in between the head of Riley's mattress and the foot of ours.

The boys are disappointed that we're not in the apartment. I point out that our toolshed offers the perfect conditions for night-time storytelling, and Aidan's grumbling stops. Small things make him happy, it's a gift. Riley's mood is harder to shift: he's quiet and hiding his face.

'What is it, sweetheart?' I ask. He's reluctant to say, so I suggest Shannon and Aidan go up to the kitchen and put the kettle on for afternoon tea. 'I'm sure I could smell apple cake when we got out of the van.'

Aidan is down the ladder before I've finished the sentence.

'Is there something bothering you?' I ask Riley, when we're alone.

'I just wish we were in the apartment,' Riley says in a low, defeated voice.

'We all do, darling, but it isn't available. The people staying in the apartments are paying guests, so even Simona and Amalie can't live in them at the moment.' Riley is staring at his hands; he still hasn't met my eyes. 'What is it you miss so much about the apartment?'

'The toilet.' He's so quiet I can barely hear him.

'The toilet? But we're not as far from the toilet here as we were at the woodhouse, and at night you have your very own ensuite.' I flourish my hand toward the bucket, but it fails to amuse.

'But I can't use it properly.'

'The bucket? All you have to do is aim.'

'No, the other toilet, the one in the ground. It's too wide for me and I sometimes fall in.'

Oh. The things they keep to themselves. The other toilet, the one we've been told to use, has two porcelain footrests either side of a hole in the ground. The width between them is perfect for an adult but, I realise now, too far apart for a small nine-year-old boy. The daily fear of falling in your own shit – we had no idea.

'That, my love, is easily solved. I'll have a very quiet word with Ulrike, and I'm sure she'll let you use the toilet inside the house whenever you want. Would you prefer that?'

Riley looks at me now and nods. I wrap myself around him, happy to cocoon him forever, but a craving for apple cake cuts our hug short and we join the others in the kitchen.

We fall into the routines of the farm as if we've only been away for a day or two, though there are some changes. The lingering chill of winter has gone, and the summer heat has covered the elderberry in clusters of white flowers, and the raspberry canes in fruit. Herbs fill the garden beds we rescued last time we were here, and the hothouse has been abandoned for the open field. There is so much to do, and we're eager to help.

Honey has been a priority in recent weeks. Acacia blossoms have been transformed into gold by Stefan's bees, and the whole family has spent twelve hours a day separating it from the debris of the hives. We've arrived just in time to pour the clean honey into jars. When we tire of that, there is plenty to do in the fields; they have been neglected during the honey harvest and there are all manner of things to plant, prune and pick.

The last WWOOFer planted tomato seedlings, which are now searching for something to climb. And we're given the job of building the frames. Stefan stands with us at the head of the first two rows.

'He did not really understand how to keep them straight,' Stefan is saying. 'He has not grown anything before and he pulled much out that should have stayed in, and put much in that will not grow well, but he was a good WWOOFer.' Stefan is smiling, humoured by the wonky rows.

'What made him a good WWOOFer?' I ask.

'He cared about what he was doing; he tried. He is not used to this life, but he wanted to learn.' Stefan turns to me and chuckles. 'He is now living nearby with other young people, in a communal house, and is showing them how to grow food. It won't matter if the rows are not straight.'

'But it must be more work for you, to have WWOOFers who don't know a tomato from a weed?' I suddenly remember all the perfectly productive raspberry canes I snipped off last time I was here and wish I'd kept my mouth shut.

'Yes, it is more work.' He looks to Shannon and pats him on the shoulder, 'It is not usual to have someone like Shannon. But everyone brings something with them when they come, and if they leave with some knowledge of growing food, this is good, and maybe better than perfect rows of tomatoes.'

Stefan is confident we can do this job without him. Shannon is confident we can do this job without him. I am confident I can follow Shannon's instructions. But Stefan wants things done differently to Lauren – instead of a single row of vertical frames, he uses a traditional A-frame construction between two rows.

Shannon and I work beside each other, forcing long, thin chestnut branches into the dry soil and tying them in pairs near the top. We discuss the merits of both types of frame. I think the A-frame is easier to construct and looks better, but Shannon suspects it might encourage disease as the plants touch at the top and airflow around them is reduced. He decides Lauren's vertical frames are probably more productive, though concedes that they're a bit more work to build. We clearly have different priorities.

The boys find us when they want us. We haven't seen them for hours, but I feel none of the angst I did at *Pirapora*. When we left them after breakfast they were planning to head down to the river with Marta.

'It's still really cold in the water, but there are heaps of tadpoles. Ulrike gave us a bucket and we've been collecting them.' Aidan is animated, bare feet, bare chest. 'Will you come down?'

'How about we all go down for a swim after lunch,' Shannon suggests.

'When is lunch? I'm hungry,' Riley says.

I look at my watch, it's one o'clock. 'It might be an hour away, shall I get you a snack?'

I think back to our first visit – the long, famished hours waiting to be fed, our shyness and reluctance to intrude or be a burden. We've learnt a lot since then. Not only how to fit in with this family and its rhythms, but how to assert our own. We've gained a confidence that I didn't realise we lacked until we came to Italy. Our lives back home are so independent that we floundered when we came here – we didn't know how to be ourselves in another family's home. Now, we move comfortably around the farm and the family. We help ourselves when we're hungry or when a cup of tea is required; we find out what needs to be done and we weave time around it in a way that works for everyone. I find I'm not planning ahead as much, so the anxiety of not getting things done has disappeared.

Lunch is as we remember it, though the heat of summer has moved it out of the kitchen and into the shade of the cherry tree. Marta and Aidan eat quickly so they can test their limits on the swing. Riley hovers around Amalie, scooping her up every time she ventures in the path of the human pendulum. When Simona takes Amalie to the woodhouse for a nap and Ulrike retreats inside the house for her repose, we suggest that Marta join us down at the river for a swim.

'Bracing' is one word for it, though 'freezing' might be more accurate. The river has lost its urgency in the dry of summer, but not its bite. Marta is braver than the rest of us and has submerged herself in the deep pool that catches the water coming down from the mountain. I'm determined to get my hair wet, but it leaves me gasping and I scramble to a large flat rock to recline and recover. The boys have sacrificed all feeling in their legs to wade through the water catching fat tadpoles in their hands and storing them in a bucket for indefinite observation. It becomes a game that we all play, seeing how many of the slippery wrigglers we can keep hold of in the cupped traps of our hands.

Shannon goes to find Stefan at the old mill, leaving us to frolic. When I join them half an hour later, they're discussing Shannon's next job.

The mill was decommissioned years ago and the reservoir that fed the water-wheel was turned into a swimming pool, but it's been losing water. A small stone wall needs to be built at the point where river water was once channelled into the reservoir. It's a big job, but Shannon has built stone walls before. He and Stefan are working out the best approach, and they take it in turns to talk, nodding and laughing in unison. If you didn't know who was host and who was WWOOFer, you wouldn't easily work it out.

~

Before dinner, the boys and I wander down the path past the honey room, past our Turkish toilet, past the herb garden and along the top of the vegetable field where the frames we constructed are braced for the weight of hundreds of tomatoes. At the end of the path is a field of raspberries.

Every day we collect kilos of berries. We eat as much as we like and still fill our baskets to overflowing. This is what it would feel like to win a golden ticket and find yourself in Willy Wonka's chocolate factory. This is what the *River Cottage* and *Gourmet Farmer* have promised. But now I know how much work makes it real.

Ulrike and I got to know each other amongst these raspberry canes. The hours we spent shuffling along the aisles between the rows were back-breaking and left me with a rash on both arms from the fine hairs on the plants, but the company made up for it. It's been the greatest pleasure to return and see the fruits of all that labour.

This evening Ulrike joins us amongst the raspberries, and we pick up where we left off, talking about children, our gentle men, and WWOOFing on another farm.

'We never really became friends,' I say when the subject turns to Lauren. 'I think she saw us as a source of labour but nothing more, so it was difficult to settle in.'

'People want different things from this experience,' Ulrike says. 'Sometimes they want too much.'

I hope she's talking about Lauren, but suspect she's talking about me.

When our baskets are full we carry them up to the kitchen. Ulrike puts half of them in a large pot, adds sugar and lights the stove. The rest go in bags to be frozen. This has happened every day since we arrived, and jars of jam are piling up on shelves in the cellar. There might be a hundred by the time the vines stop producing.

At breakfast this morning, Stefan told me they'll only last a few months.

'Surely longer than that,' I'd said. Then I watched him use a dessert spoon to dollop the crimson jam on his porridge. The boys took note, and by the end of breakfast a whole jar was empty.

~

I think we might be working more than we did the first time we were here, but it feels easier. It's late morning. The boys and Marta have just delivered three baskets of raspberries to the kitchen where I'm preparing bread, and Ulrike is scrubbing potatoes for lunch – we're working like an extended family, and I'm conscious of how true it is that many hands make light work.

The children help themselves to thick slices of apple cake, straight from the baking tray, then find the Monopoly board and head outside. I follow with tins of wet dough – like the children, it needs time in the sun to grow. When I've placed the last tin on the table I pause to listen to Marta translating a Chance card for Aidan. They're comfortable and settled, so I decide to visit Shannon down at the old mill pool.

The weather is hot, but the woods are perpetually cool. The contrast raises goosebumps on my skin and I hug myself to clear them. Branches from mature chestnut trees reach over the path like protective arms in an enchanted forest. It's all I can do to stop myself skipping, and then I realise there's no reason not to, so I skip.

The wall is well underway. Shannon's been at it all morning.

'Feel like a break?' I say.

He unfurls and leans back as far as he can, holding his fists into the small of his back.

'I've brought cake.' I have him now. He loves the ritual of a tea break after hours of hard work. This is what we are both good at – him, the hard work; me, the distraction.

'Your timing is perfect. I'm starving.'

I feel I've done a good thing, bringing this man sustenance.

'My legs need a stretch. Why don't we walk to the old pig house?' he says.

'What girl could refuse such an offer?'

The pig house has recently had a stone and terracotta floor laid and will soon be another option for accommodation. We step over the threshold into its cool interior – such a relief from the heat outside.

There's nowhere to sit, so Shannon rests against a wall and finishes his cake. I lean my arms on the wide sill of a small window and look out at the woods that would claim this small building if it was ignored for more than a few months. The thought amuses me.

'What are you smiling about?' Shannon is whispering into my neck. His arms have wrapped around me and his fingers have tucked themselves between mine.

'I'm imagining all those rows of carrots at *Pirapora*.'

'What about them?'

'They'd be smothered in weeds by now.'

'Probably.'

'I wonder how we'll go with just the two of us?'

'Mm.'

He isn't listening, why would he be? This is the first time we've been out of earshot of the boys for weeks. I turn around and his lips catch mine. There's nothing to lie on, so we stay standing up. We improvise.

~

'You are a baker now, when you leave you must take some *pasta madre*.'

Ulrike is offering me her mother dough, the bread starter she's been nurturing for years. To me, this *pasta madre* is a part of her – part of this place and way of life. I interpret her gift as a vote of confidence, and suddenly I realise how much I've wanted a sign that I might have what it takes to live this good life. It's the night before we leave again and I'm emotional. When I finally get a hold of myself, my thoughts have come full circle – Ulrike would never presume to judge my worthiness, for a good life or anything else. She's offering me something she's noticed gives me pleasure. She is kind. Why should I seek more than that from anyone?

When Shannon comes into the kitchen Ulrike and I are trying to figure out the best way to package the *pasta madre* so it survives the trip home.

'You won't be able to get it through Australian quarantine, even if it does survive until then.' Shannon is ever practical.

'Maybe you can send it by post,' Ulrike suggests. She doesn't understand why Australian quarantine would have a problem with her gift, and I'm so taken with the idea of baking Ulrike's bread in my kitchen that I let her convince me it will be okay.

We decide the only way to preserve the starter will be to dry it. I can then reconstitute it when I get home, feed it with fresh rye flour and water for a few days until it is active again. Ulrike goes to the fridge and gets out the raw dough left over from the loaves I made the other day. She scoops out half.

'Will you have enough left for your own bread?' I ask.

'It does not need much. And I think you will need a little more because of the drying.'

She spreads it thin on a sheet of foil, and I take it out to sit in the hot afternoon sun.

~

Long trestle tables fill the community hall in the nearby village of Faltona. It's the annual pizza-fest, and it coincides with our last night at *Il Mulino*. Almost every seat is taken, and we're ushered out onto the balcony by a young woman in a bright orange T-shirt – the uniform for the army of pizza bearers bringing cheers from lucky tables receiving food.

The menu is a long list of pizzas. We tick our favourites and line up to pay the cashier. I can see Stefan in the kitchen behind the counter. He's pushing a pizza into a brick oven with a long-handled oven peel. It slides off without incident and he reaches for another. Eight people are at various stations: an old man is shredding mozzarella in what looks like a meat mincer, one woman is forming balls of dough and another is putting them through a roller to create the round pizza bases. She passes them to the central table where five people are turning our pizza dreams into reality. Stefan is the last port of call.

When he pulls out a cooked pizza, cheese still bubbling, the base slightly charred around the edges, I catch his eye. As always, he smiles gently and tilts his head. As always, I blush.

All the people from this village and its surrounds must have turned up tonight. Everyone knows everyone and we, with our awkward Italian, are curiosities. It's easy to long for this kind of community, but it's also easy to romanticise it. Half the young people have come home for the weekend from the cities where they work or study. Most of them won't return to live here. The revelry and good cheer tonight is as much about seeing family and old friends as it is about the food.

By the time we've eaten every last delicious crumb of our pizzas, the hall is almost empty. I watch as Stefan farewells the few who've stayed behind to clean up. Each time, he smiles and tilts his head, and I see my affection for him in their eyes. When his white van disappears down the hill, I feel as if I've been left alone at the dance.

The four of us squeeze into the car of a friend and drive the dark roads back to the farm. When we're dropped off we stand in the dark, invisible and watching. The kitchen light is on and we can see Stefan and Ulrike moving around the table. Ulrike has laid it with bread, and Stefan is taking raspberry jam from the fridge. They sit down with Marta for a midnight snack. This time alone would be rare.

'Why don't we leave them to it?' I say to Shannon.

'Good idea.' He finds my hand and we start down the path to the toolshed. Then Riley calls out in a panic.

'Dad! Mum!'

We turn around to look into the darkness.

'What is it, Riley?' Shannon asks.

'Stefan's van. It's flooding!'

Riley points behind him. The white van is spectral in the moonlight, but we can't see anything amiss. Aidan is the first to get to it, and the grin on his face communicates a mishap of entertaining proportions for a twelve-year-old boy.

When I reach the van my hand automatically covers my mouth. 'Oh my god,' I say into it. 'Quick, Riley. Run and tell Stefan.'

Riley races towards the lighted kitchen, and I wish that we were able to deal with this disaster ourselves. Shannon goes to the van doors and pulls them open. Water gushes out.

It's Aidan who discovers the source of the calamity. 'There's a hose filling up one of the drums in the back.'

Shannon traces its serpentine tail to a tap. When the water is turned off we see the neck of the hose sag, and the curtain of water that's been falling from the drum and filling the van stills.

We follow Riley into the kitchen. Stefan's holding a slice of rye bread thickly spread with jam. He's finishing a mouthful before responding to Riley's alarming message.

'No matter,' he says, gently shaking his head. Riley looks at us dumbfounded, afraid he's been misunderstood and appealing to one of us to reinforce the bad news.

'The whole van is flooded, Stefan. I'm not sure what the damage is,' says Shannon.

'Has the hose been shut?' He asks, raising the bread and jam to his mouth and making no move to push his chair out and run to the scene of destruction.

'Yes, I turned it off.'

'Then it is done. I will look at it in the morning.' He motions for us to sit. Neither Marta nor Ulrike seem concerned about the van, or our intrusion, so we join them.

I lean into Shannon. 'The Zen of Stefan,' I whisper. He smiles in agreement.

~

As a farewell gift, Ulrike presents us with one precious jar of jam and six jars of honey. Unable to say no – because we're polite or greedy, it's hard to decide – we wrap them in clothes. We're thinking of the week ahead, to be spent in an apartment in Lucca. We're looking forward to raspberry jam on toast and porridge, and honey by the spoonful.

'Next time you come, you are our guests. No work.' Stefan's smile is broad now, like the open door of their lighted kitchen. It's our second farewell, and maybe, because of that, it feels less painful. We came back once, why wouldn't we come back again?

The whole family is there to see us off. We hold each other with affection. Simona and I write down email addresses – we want her to visit us in Australia. Marta could come in a few years, and Amalie when she's older: we're full of the possibilities. But I've travelled enough to know that these plans often fade, that the intimacy of travel is fragile. Right now, the thought of losing these relationships to time seems impossible.

We get into the van. It's damp, but otherwise unharmed. Stefan drives us all the way to Arezzo on the pretext of having to check hives somewhere in the vicinity. Maybe he does, or maybe it's just a convenience that allows for his kindness. It gives us another hour together.

When the van drives away from the station we watch it until it rounds a corner and is gone. Shannon turns to me and pulls something from behind his back.

'I found this when I was helping Stefan clean out the van.'

It's my hat, miraculously dry thanks to its hiding place high amongst the piled-up hives. I hold it to my nose. It smells of honey, of *Il Mulino*, and of Stefan. Each of us takes our memories and unlikely fancies to platform four, and we wait for the train to Lucca.

Lucca
(Pay attention)

Damiano is waiting for us – his motorcycle and his gun steal the boys' attentions, his tight pants and high leather boots steal mine. It's an unexpected encounter with a member of Italy's *polizia*, and when he offers his hand and welcomes us in halting English, only Shannon is able to speak coherently. Introductions are made, then Damiano ushers us into his pride and joy.

The apartment is disappointingly modern.

'You are the first to stay here,' he says, after we've carefully placed our packs on the polished timber floor. 'I hope it is as you like.' His smile is that of a child offering you the first taste of a cake he's made himself.

'It's perfect,' I say, casting an uneasy eye over the black leather couch and the metallic blue bedspread shining beyond the bedroom door.

'In the cupboards is everything you need. But if it is not, you must telephone me and I will bring it.' The cupboards are white and glossy, and he opens each in turn to reveal a coffee machine, a food processor, a juicer and various appliances I can't identify. I see my scowling face reflected briefly as he closes the last door.

What complicated standards I have, I think. I'm thrilled to have an ensuite and a coffee machine, but I want it all wrapped up in stone and terracotta, not brick veneer and stainless steel. An image of refugees bathing at a drinking fountain slaps away my complaint.

'It's perfect,' I say again to Damiano, and I mean it this time. He's delighted, and we hand over a week's rent.

The boys have a different aesthetic to me. When the front door clicks shut, they marvel at the fridge hidden so cleverly inside a cupboard; the bathroom so big and bright-red; the floor so slippery they can slide across it in their socked feet. Then there's the television, wide and flat, and the large remote control perched precisely on the square arm of the black couch. With exaggerated sweetness they appeal to us for permission to press its red button.

Since leaving Australia, a television has become a cause of celebration for the boys. They don't seem to miss it when we're on a farm – it's out of sight and out of mind – but when they see one, the possibilities for colour and comedy and the contained chaos of make-believe are too much to resist. When the screen lights up, Shannon and I retreat for a nap.

We wake to find the boys watching *Wacky Races*.

'I found an English cartoon channel,' Aidan tells us, bouncing up and down in the way he does when delighted.

We squeeze in between them on the couch and spend the next couple of hours steeped in the programs of our own childhoods.

We watch *Scooby-Doo* then *Road Runner*. Between *The Jetsons* and *The Flintstones* I hand around what's left of the biscuits we packed for the train. When *Wacky Races* comes on again we all start laughing like Muttley, the dog. It's a bonding experience, one of the reasons we came to Italy, but I never thought it would happen in front of a screen. I can't work out if this is a triumph or a failure. *Josie and the Pussy Cats* comes on and I suggest a walk. The boys have no interest in shapely cartoon women dressed in skimpy cat suits, so they agree.

There's nothing really to see in Lucca, but everything to notice. The town is wrapped in a thick cloak of stone, protection against admirers from the sixteenth century. These walls were impenetrable then, but are inviting now, having been transformed from a battlement into a boulevard.

We circumnavigate the four-kilometre wall and introduce ourselves slowly to the city within. Nothing stands out. Like so many Italian cities, Lucca is a patchwork of terracotta and stucco broken only by the varied green of private gardens and the occasional public park. Her buildings sit comfortably side by side – the grand not too grand, the humble not shy. When the sun falls behind the Apuan Alps the boys become silhouettes against the paling sky.

~

With no chores or masters, our first few days in Lucca have been passed in slow motion. Today we let the children lead the way, and they take us along the canal that divides *Via del Fosso*.

There are no footpaths here, we share the road with bicycles and a few cars, and everything moves at human pace. An old man – white apron over a Buddha belly – sweeps the road outside his *alimentari*, and I'm struck by the fastidiousness of his shopkeeping. *How often does he tend to this part of the road?* I think. Is it boredom or pride, or is it the need to be convivial?

'*Buongiorno, signora.*' He straightens and leans on his broom. There's no pile of dirt that I can see.

'*Buongiorno, signore,*' I respond. The shop behind him tempts me in. I ask the boys if they're hungry, they nod and I steer them through the doorway.

Inside seems dark after the bright of day, and the small space is filled with the colours and textures of pasta, bread, cured meats and fresh sauces. They obscure the windows and crowd the floor. The old man squeezes his belly past us and stands behind the counter, waiting while the boys make up their minds. They ask in timid voices for *panino* – Riley wants *formaggio dolce con prosciutto*. Aidan wants *morta'della*, 'without the peppercorns,' he says in English.

They've tried, and are rewarded with a stream of words, incomprehensible but all turned up at the edges like audible smiles. They accept the praise and watch as their panini are expertly split and filled with more than they can safely hold. An origami wrap, then I'm asked for three euros. Not enough, I gesture. More than enough, smiles the Buddha. He follows us out of the shop, broom in hand, and we continue along the canal.

'Listen,' I say, and we all stop walking. A soprano is scaling the alphabet.

La, la, la, la, la, la, la. Then, silence.

We keep walking, but before we've reached the end of *Via del Fosso*, we hear her again – one long note, five shorter notes. It's a familiar beginning, even for someone who's never been to the opera. We stop and lean against the low brick wall of the canal. I wonder if she knows we're listening, if she's looking out of her window like Madam Butterfly looked out of hers. We stay to listen to every note, barely moving, even when she wavers. I imagine all the others, in their kitchens and their bedrooms in the apartments either side of hers, our Buddha sweeping the road that doesn't need sweeping. All of them listening. I bow my head and wait for her voice to come high and strong along the canal, and when it does, my breath catches unexpectedly in my chest. The longing in the final drawn-out notes is so familiar.

'Mum's crying!' Riley announces.

Startled, I wipe at my eyes. 'I'm not crying, I'm just moved,' I say, as Shannon puts an arm around my shoulders. Before he can ask anything I change the subject. 'Maybe we can go to an opera recital while we're here, after all, this is where Puccini was born, and you kids really should know more about music than you do.'

'That would be very ... educational,' Shannon says, giving my shoulder a playful squeeze. 'And not at all boring for the boys.'

'Who's Puccini?' Riley asks.

I give Shannon the smuggest look I can muster. 'Puccini was a composer, and in 1904 he wrote the music we were just listening to.'

'How do you even know that?' Shannon asks.

'I read it in the guide book this morning.'

'If *you* didn't know it when you were our age, why do *we* need to know it now?' asks Aidan.

I look to Shannon for backup. He gives me the smuggest look he can muster.

We take a serpentine route to nowhere in particular and end up on *Via Sant' Andrea*.

'Wow, how cool is that?' Aidan has stopped walking and is looking up. He's noticed, high above us, a tower topped with trees. We can't find anything about it in our travel guide, but it's open to the public and can be climbed for a few euros. The boys aren't interested in the climb: it's enough for them to crane their necks and marvel at the garden in the sky from below. A brief tussle ensues where I metaphorically shove them up the steep stairs of the tower towards some nebulous educational experience, and they metaphorically shut their eyes and stick their fingers in their ears. I lose this battle of wills. The winners get gelato, while Shannon and I tuck the tower away for a child-free afternoon.

~

A few days later and we've left the boys in the very capable hands of Nanny (our affectionate name for the television) and a box of biscotti. They were thrilled, and so were we. All this family time is interfering with their screen life, and our love life – we all need an afternoon to rediscover the magic.

Shannon and I hold hands along the canal and take the same circuitous route as the other day.

'What do you love most?' I ask.

'About Lucca?'

'Yes.'

'The separate bedroom.'

'We could have that anywhere.'

'We could, but we don't, so that gets all my votes.' He exaggerates a wink. 'What about you?'

'I love watching all the people go about their lives – there's none of the agitation you get in other cities. Lucca's like a happy hive. I reckon I could live here.'

'You just want to be one of those worker bees who flies out each day in search of the best coffee shop then goes back to tell the rest.'

'I reckon I'd be good at that job.'

'I reckon you'd be brilliant.' We stop walking and Shannon points up, 'There it is.'

The *Torre Guinigi* is one of just a few remaining towers in Lucca. At the time of its erection (there really isn't a better word for it) there were two hundred and fifty similar towers of various sizes, commissioned by the alpha males of 14th and 15th century Lucca. *Torre Guinigi* was impressive, even back then. The Guinigi family had seven sons and topped their tower with seven oaks.

The tower is a sight, of sorts, but it's no Colosseum – more a quirky landmark that asks for no more than a pause and a comment from its visitors. But like the city's wall, it invites you up to share the view. It's this gentle drawing-in that I love about Lucca. Unlike Rome, where the sites have celebrity status and demand to be seen, there's no insistence here, no bragging, no vanity. Lucca is accessible, and if you smile at her, she'll smile back. It's impossible to be disappointed.

The ascent is dizzying. Hundreds of stairs spiral up through the centre of the redbrick tower and I'm thankful for the occasional landing, each with its own unique view of the city. A ladder takes us the last few metres and we emerge into what could be a courtyard garden. The trees we're standing under aren't the ones planted by the Guinigi family, but my pamphlet tells me they're hundreds of years old. Shallow soil and exposure has kept their trunks thin, but they create a dense canopy, and I enjoy the shade.

'I like this garden. You could plant seven fruit trees, instead of seven oaks, and it wouldn't take much effort to weed,' I say.

'That's true. But it wouldn't feed you much, and it certainly wouldn't make you a living.'

'Do you think that's a real possibility, making a living off our land?'

'I think it is, if we both give it our full attention.'

I've heard this before, and it doesn't bode well. The last time Shannon suggested that all I needed to do was give something my full attention was when I called him at work and asked him to 'remind me what is so fucking good about slow living'.

177

He fumbled with his phone, not because of my language but because his hands were numb from cold after a morning of gardening in the rain.

I'd negotiated to work from home every Monday and found myself in a weekly struggle with our fireplace, my only source of heat during the chilly Hills winter. My approach was characteristically efficient, or so I thought. I'd start with a layer of scrunched-up newspaper, carefully arrange twigs on top in a crosshatch pattern – multiple layers for maximum ignition – then I'd add larger and larger sticks until finally I'd place a good-sized log on top. Only then would I take my match and strike. Ah, the joy of seeing the flames leap up. For a minute I'd sit and watch them grow, then I'd begin my day's work. This process took about five minutes if all the bits were waiting in the basket by the fireplace (and a little elf always ensured they were), and for me, five minutes was a small price to pay for the comfort and aesthetic of a crackling fire and that primal satisfaction of having created heat from the basic material offered up by our land.

But it was not a fairytale with a happy ending. I'd tell myself to check the fire in a few minutes, then let an hour pass into the black hole of email before jumping from my chair in panic. In retrospect this part of my morning replays in slow motion. The anguish shows on my face as my head slowly turns towards the fireplace; it changes to despair as I realise there's no flame, then anger at my neglect and, finally, resignation as I pull on my gumboots and beanie and head out to the wood shed to saw up wood. I can't say I conducted myself with grace at these times: I'd swear and kick things, and in my darkest moments

I'd devise ways of smuggling an energy-hungry electric radiator into the house for my own personal use – it could be my dirty little secret.

Some time later, cold and damp, I'd stagger back into the house with an armful of wood, kneel down at the fireplace and practically sob when it was clear I'd used up all my kindling. Bits of paper would be twisted into twig-like shapes and I'd pile them in, add the wood and strike a match. When it caught I'd sit vigilant until the larger logs had succumbed to the flame. Only then would I return to work – two hours after I'd built the original fire.

On the day I called Shannon, the wood had been too damp and my second fire had smouldered and gone out. I was ready to give up on the whole thing.

'You're rushing it,' he said. 'You need to give it all your attention until it's blazing. Believe it or not, you'll waste less time if you go slowly.'

'So what am I supposed to do now?'

'Put on an extra jumper.'

When he got home that night, I watched him light the fire – three bits of paper and a handful of salvaged twigs, then strike. There was no inferno, just a small flame, but Shannon watched it, nurtured it, gave it his full attention. In about six minutes it was blazing. We could forget all about it while we got dinner ready and by the time we sat down to eat, the house was toasty.

Now I turn away from the oak trees and look out to the hills rising up beyond Lucca's walls. Shannon's right: we can make it work if we give it our full attention. But my mind has always been inclined to wander, and right now I can't keep the life we've planned in focus. I feel the emotion of hearing the opera singer the other day tightening my chest. Puccini's music and an image of a woman waiting for her life to begin have roused a longing, and a fear. Neither of which I want to examine right now.

'Remind me, have we got the time and money for a glass of wine and a plate of cheese before we relieve Nanny of her duties?' I ask.

'You're dreaming if you think we can afford cheese,' says Shannon. 'But I can offer you a glass of wine and a beautiful view.'

'That's good enough,' I say, and I lead the way back down to earth.

~

Chiesa di San Giovanni is built of white marble, and we enter through detailed brass doors. The interior is cool, as with all these old churches. Stories of Christ colour the walls, there's a frescoed dome and a ceiling of golden honeycomb. But where the altar once stood, there's now a grand piano on factory-cut terracotta pavers, and images of Christ are hidden behind images of Puccini, printed in black and white on larger-than-life banners. He's sacred to the Luccans, and makes this deconsecrated church a place of worship again.

We've come early so we can see the Roman ruins that this church was built on. We walk around the rows of plastic chairs set out for the recital and descend a metal staircase to the archaeological site. Below the precisely cut marble columns of the 12th-century church are 1st-century pillars of roughly hewn stone. A mosaic floor emerges from the sediment, as bright and beautiful as the day it was laid. The blue of the larger tiles is the same as some of the tiles we collected on the beach in Calabria. I wonder if objects can capture time, if they can store traces of life, like memories, in their molecular structure. It's not the first time I've heard the breath of history whispering in my ear. I feel her hand guiding mine as I reach beyond the metal bars to stroke the surface of a tile that I'm sure, in this moment, a woman of Rome once absently stroked to calm her troubled mind. The tiles are smooth and cold; if there's life in them they're reluctant to share it. Shannon and the boys tread heavily on the metal walkway that hovers above the mosaic, and I can feel the vibrations of their footsteps through my whole body. Someone starts warming up at the piano.

Puccini features heavily in our musical hour. A male pianist accompanies two sopranos: one young and promising, the other mature and accomplished. Surprisingly (satisfyingly) the boys are as transfixed as we are. It's the closeness of the musicians, and the occasional frailty of the young woman's voice, her brow creasing in moments of anxiety. We all want her to reach and hold the higher notes. Aidan wonders if she's the one we heard practising the other day. 'Maybe,' I say. She bows, her smile more relaxed now that her solo is over, and the older woman returns.

She sings *'Un bel di vedremo'* from Madam Butterfly. Riley recognises it, and in my peripheral vision I see him turn to search my face for confirmation. But I can't look away from the woman singing. I'm trying to slow down every note. I want to turn the minutes into hours and the hours into days. I realise that I've found that part of Italy I could easily call home, and if I thought even one of my boys would agree, I would suggest we stay a while longer, rent an old apartment on *Via del Fosso*, and get used to the music of Puccini. I struggle to make sense of the desire I have for this city. It feels as if it's directed towards a person. Lucca has done nothing to deserve my adoration – she's like a beautiful woman who doesn't care how she looks, and barely notices the attentions of others. Maybe this is her secret, and her charm: she knows herself, and is authentic.

If I look at Riley, or move to wipe the tear that traces mascara down my cheek, it will all end too soon. Riley takes my hand and squeezes it. This is our farewell.

Emilia-Romagna

(Don't worry)

———

Most of the people on this train are headed for Bologna, but a few get off with us at Pianoro. They soon disperse, and we're left alone at the station. We find a bench with a view of the car park and get out the sandwiches we made before leaving Lucca. They've gone soggy in the heat, and so have we.

There's a distinct lack of enthusiasm for this next farm. We grew accustomed to the comforts of our apartment and our lazy routines, and I'm suffering from what feels like the depression of an unrequited love. It's absurd, I know, but Lucca stirred up desire and made me weep, how else can I describe it? Aidan and Riley have tried to negotiate a revision of our rules of engagement with other children – if they are annoying or too bossy the boys want permission to employ avoidance tactics. Ideally this would involve long hours in our room with their DSs, but they're also willing to hang out with us, as long as they don't have to do too much work. We've said we'll think about it. Shannon and I are nervous that a difficult experience on this farm will bring a chorus of dissent, and agitation to move on or go home. We can't afford to move on, and we don't want to go home. But our month in Calabria has made us wary and raised questions about what this journey means for the boys – and, if I'm honest, what it means for me.

I'm mid-thought and mid-sandwich when a tired-looking Subaru drives into the empty car park. Two young women get out, go around to the back and open the boot. The driver, a woman not much younger than me, helps them to drag out their packs, embracing them in turn and smiling with such affection that I can only assume they're family.

I must be staring. The woman sees me and waves.

'Do you think that's Elisa?' Shannon says.

'She's not due for another twenty minutes.'

The woman is looking at us, waving again. She's wearing cut-off denim shorts and a singlet. All of her limbs are long and tanned and smooth, her hair is short and practical, her smile and her eyes are bright and easy, and she wears no make-up or jewellery. She's beautiful, but it's of no consequence to her – Lucca in human form.

I put my sandwich down and go over, butterflies flitting in my stomach. 'Elisa?'

'Yes, you must be Pip.' She leans in and kisses both my cheeks. Then she introduces me to the young women who are struggling to shoulder their heavy packs.

'They have been with us for two weeks. We will miss them.' She smiles again, a broad smile that lifts the corners of her large blue eyes.

The women are American college students on their summer break. As one, they begin a string of high-pitched testimonials about WWOOFing at *Il Granello*. 'You'll just love it,' they say. 'They're the best, and the kids are so cute, and Henry …' At this point there's a pause and a giggle. I take the opportunity to call Shannon and the boys over with our luggage.

The road from Pianoro winds steadily up hill, past woods and the occasional farmhouse, and eventually into the village of Livergnano. There's a uniformity about the buildings, and Elisa tells us that almost every house was destroyed towards the end of World War II. I try to imagine what a bombardment would sound like, but I have no reference point, thank goodness. We turn left and travel up and over a hill, leaving behind the main street and its faded war. A rough descent leads directly to *Il Granello*.

The road cuts the property in half – the house is on the right, the barn on the left and rows of herbs and vegetables flank each side. If we drove another fifty metres we'd be in the courtyard of a stone building as old and beautiful as any we've seen in Lucca.

'That's the old monastery,' Elisa says. 'The nuns believed God kept it safe during the war, but really, it was physics.' She parks the car, but we wait for an explanation before getting out. 'Missiles were launched from the other side of the escarpment. The trajectory they needed to clear the cliffs meant they landed just a few metres beyond the monastery. The escarpment saved it – though I guess God had a hand in its formation.'

We unload our packs and dance through the farm's menagerie. Four dogs crowd in on us, countless chickens scatter in our wake and two goats manoeuvre around a pony for a better view of the new wwooFers. Aidan is trying to make friends with them all when he spies a more interesting creature beyond a fence.

'Who's that?' he asks.

'That is Pancetta, the pig,' replies Elisa.

'That's a funny name for a pig. It's like calling it bacon.' Finally, he's learning Italian.

'We wanted her to be bacon, but now we can't do it. We all love her too much.'

'She's kind of ugly, isn't she?' Aidan is crouching down now, with his fingers wriggling through the fence. Pancetta is small, standing no taller than thirty centimetres on stubby legs that barely keep her belly from brushing the ground. Patchy black hair reveals grey skin beneath, and Elisa tells Aidan that the bald patches all over her face are the result of sunburn.

'That's why we built her a shelter,' she says. 'Would you like to be in charge of giving her breakfast while you're here?'

Aidan's smile is as broad and bright as Elisa's. She puts a hand on his shoulder and asks if he and Riley would like to meet her children. In that instant, we feel at home.

The farmhouse is large and industrial – three floors with bars on the windows and a look of benign neglect. Inside the heavy front door there's a kitchen to our left and an all-purpose room to our right. At the back is a huge fireplace harbouring the remains of a fire – absurd, given the heat of the day. In the centre is a long table strewn with paper and coloured pencils and children.

There are three. A boy is hunched over a drawing, his face serious and intent. He looks about Riley's age, and I recognise the same gentle quietness. A girl lies along the table with long, thin limbs. Straight brown hair falls either side of her delicate face, and when she looks at us, it's with her mother's eyes, large and blue like the Mediterranean. Watching them both is a small boy. He's fair haired and blue eyed but has the same honeyed skin as his siblings. They fit together, these three. If Elisa told me they never fought, I'd believe her.

Elisa speaks to them in Italian, then turns to our boys. 'Aidan and Riley, this is Lorenzo, he is nine years old. This is Alice, she is eight. And this little one is Gabri, he will be six years old next week.' Gabri beams at her, Lorenzo and Alice offer quiet greetings in Italian. They are shy, seeking confirmation from their mother that they've done enough to welcome us. Instead of pushing them she guides us into the kitchen, where Romano and the other two WWOOFers are preparing lunch.

Romano's eyes are dark, like Lorenzo's, and they twinkle. I'm not sure I've ever seen a twinkle in someone's eye until now, but it's definitely there, below the thick eyebrows and above the greying beard. He takes Shannon's hand in a friendly shake then bends slightly to extend the same courtesy to the boys. Finally, his whiskers are against my cheek.

~

In the early evening we help carry food to the table in the back garden. Wine is poured, a pot of pasta with tomato sauce is passed from hand to hand, olive oil is drizzled on fresh bread. We get to know one another.

Henry: twenty-one, dreadlocks, tattoos, and a ring through his lip. He's studying Italian at a university in the UK and is here for six months to immerse himself in the language. The children hang off him like he's a favourite uncle, and he never fails to give them his attention. After four months with this family he can tease and make jokes in Italian, and they're all smiles.

Patti: American, older, retired, surprised she had the guts to become a WWOOFer, and absolutely delighted. She'd never even grown parsley before coming here, but wanted to have an adventure. Her eyes glisten when she tells us how much she'll miss this place when she leaves next week. Henry puts his arm around her shoulder and tells us she's teaching him to play the ukulele. Patti says he's a natural, and rests her head against him.

'How long have you been here, Romano?' Shannon asks.

'Five years. This is our dream, but it took us a long time to find the right place. And it has taken some time to make it work. This house was almost derelict when we found it – no electricity and poor plumbing. We have fixed it to live in, so the owner rents it to us for a bit less.'

The children drift away from the table, far more interested in playing with a litter of kittens than listening to the dreams of adults and the detail of making them real. Henry piles up plates and goes into the kitchen to make coffee.

Romano and Elisa tell their story. They pass the details back and forth, each interested in the other's interpretation of their life, as if it's the first time they've heard it.

For the last four years, from February to November, they've hosted at least four WWOOFers at any one time. Some, like Henry, have stayed for months and become part of the family, others, like us, have brought children and swelled the burden to five or six extra mouths. Henry brings a stack of small glasses and a pot of coffee. Without interrupting, he pours an inch of inky black for each of us then sits to listen to the story. Romano is describing their ambitions, and we recognise them as our own. The decisions they've made are the decisions we're contemplating. I hang on every word.

'We wanted to do something good with our life, and for the children, and we wanted to labour for something real,' he says.

Romano and Elisa live entirely off the five acres of land attached to the farmhouse. Exactly the same amount of land we have. They grow vegetables and herbs and sell them to families at their children's school, and at two weekly markets in Bologna – one organic and the other slow food. I can't imagine how they make enough to cover all the costs of a family of five, let alone the six extra people who sit around the table today.

'It is difficult,' Elisa says. 'For the first few years Romano had to keep working – he is a marine geologist so he was away from home for weeks at a time. But he was not happy and it was very hard for me, so now, just in the last few months, he has resigned and is finally a farmer.' She has her hand on his knee and he gives her a look that acknowledges a long and emotional back-story.

'How did you manage?' I ask her. I'm thinking of all the things I've never done at our place and resolve to ask Shannon to show me how to start the ride-on mower the minute we get home.

'I could only manage because of WWOOFers.'

'But WWOOFers can *create* work.'

'Yes.' She laughs. 'When we started this, I tried to be a perfect host. I thought the WWOOFers expected to have their own bathroom but we only have one for the whole house. So we rented a portable toilet and put it in the laundry, and that is what the children and Romano and I used.' Romano chuckles and Elisa pauses to take a sip of her coffee. 'I would clean the house all over before they arrived – the windows and floors, as well as their rooms. And I would cook breakfast and lunch and dinner as if it was a restaurant. It was exhausting. The children were not happy, and less work was getting done because I was in the kitchen all the time instead of in the field.' She smiles through the recollection, then notices the horror on my face and quickly reassures me. 'I do not do any of that anymore, and we are all happier – even the WWOOFers are happier. They want to be part of the family, and it is easier for everyone to relax if we share the work of cooking and cleaning.'

I want her to see relief on my face, but now I'm considering the logistics of eleven people sharing one bathroom. At least the boys will be thrilled when I suggest they take fewer showers.

~

Barking dogs and daylight wake us, but in the room next door the boys are still asleep. We steal a cuddle before rousing them then begin our descent to the kitchen. A whistled tune meets us on the landing of the first floor. It's floating up from below and Shannon and I recognise it as that '80s ear-worm 'Don't Worry, Be Happy' by Bobby McFerrin.

Romano looks up as we enter the kitchen, the whistling stops and his puckered lips stretch into a grin. 'Good morning,' he says. He asks what we like to eat for breakfast, then points to where the muesli and cornflakes are kept. 'We always keep these things for WWOOFers, but we do not eat them ourselves.' He dips a biscuit into a glass of black coffee as if to make the point.

Beside him, Lorenzo eats a wedge of cake cut from the sponge that sits in the middle of the table.

'Can I have cake for breakfast? Aidan asks.

'Yes,' I say, and we're both surprised.

The boys sit down next to Lorenzo and there's a shy exchange of greetings in Italian. Then Lorenzo passes the cake along with a few extra words they don't understand. They say *grazie*, hoping it's the correct response, and each cuts a thick slice. But Lorenzo was hoping for more. He turns to his dad, and from their quiet conversation a single word escapes that stops my boys chewing.

'... Pokémon ...'

'Lorenzo wants to know if you like Pokémon,' Romano translates.

Avoidance tactics will not be necessary, I think, and I celebrate with a slice of cake.

By eight o'clock all five children are in the main room with paper, coloured pencils and a laminating machine. Aidan and

Riley have spread the Pokémon cards they bought in Arezzo across the table, and the others are showing off their significant collection of handmade specimens. They won't miss us while we're working.

We follow Romano outside and begin our instruction on the morning routine we will inherit from the WWOOFers before us. He shows us where to find grain to feed the chickens, the ducks and the guinea fowl.

'Henry usually does this job, but it may be something the boys would like to help with,' he says. Pancetta, he explains, gets the scraps from the white bucket in the kitchen – he will show Aidan what to do later. Baskets for collecting herbs and vegetables are on a shelf just outside the front door. When full, they're stored in the cool-room beside the house.

This routine will barely change from day-to-day, but our afternoons will vary depending on the heat. Romano makes a list of the possibilities: collecting and hanging herbs, sowing seeds, packing vegetable boxes, pulverising dried herbs, mixing herb salts, collecting eggs, preparing dinner. He introduces every activity like it's one of his children – he has a soft spot for each, despite the tedium and occasional challenge. Then he mentions the figs.

'You are lucky, you have arrived at the same time as the figs.' He looks down the road, which is lined with mature trees on each side, all heavy with fruit. 'Easy money – I think that is what you say in English. We do nothing, and they grow. People will pay fifty cents for one fig. All we have to do is pick them and take them to the market.'

There's a moment of reverence for the fig, but picking them will have to wait. We grab gloves and a few baskets, and head into the vegetable field.

Elisa, Henry and Patti each have their own row. Patti is shuffling on her bum, slowly filling a basket with silverbeet. Henry's taken his shirt off, and I remember the departing WWOOFers giggling at the mention of his name. Elisa bends, stands, bends, stands. As we get closer I see her cradling great yellow blossoms in cotton-gloved hands and placing them in a foam box. They're zucchini flowers, butter-yellow and gaping wide at the sun. She suggests we harvest the zucchini, keeping the slender vegetables separate from those that are growing bulbous – they'll fetch a better price.

As the sun climbs we search the rows for vegetables of good size and colour. Our baskets fill with zucchinis: dark green and light, long and round, with flowers and without. There are only a few ripe tomatoes, but the vines are heavy with potential. Half the cucumbers have shrivelled at their ends, but we pick them regardless. They'll sell, though not for much. The eggplants aren't quite ready, and neither are the capsicums, but there's an abundance of silverbeet, and herbs of every description.

It's hot work, and I'm disappointed my back is aching so much. I go over to where Patti is sitting between two rows of silverbeet.

'The trick is to sit down and take it slowly,' she says, reminding me of Ulrike and her raspberry canes.

'That's a mantra I could definitely live by,' I say. She smiles and pats the ground beside her.

Patti shows me how to cut the silverbeet, and when we've collected enough for the market we start on the weeds.

'If these weeds had their way there'd be nothing for the market,' I say.

'That's why we're here,' says Patti. 'But it's good work, don't you think?'

I have to agree, but then I look over to Shannon. He's been trying to free a row of lettuces from the shackles of an interloping creeper and his face is overtaken by a scowl.

Romano calls from the house. The words are rhythmic and repeated. At first I can't make them out, but Patti puts down her trowel and Henry unties the T-shirt from around his head, slipping it on in a single movement as he walks towards the baskets piled with produce. He picks one up, hoists it onto his shoulder and follows the chant.

It's eleven o'clock, and this is the call to prayer. When we're all gathered in the kitchen the ceremony begins. Romano takes the espresso pot off the stove and holds it above the first small glass. No one speaks. He slowly tilts the pot, and when the coffee meets the inner curve of the spout it hisses and spits. Its venom released, Romano relaxes and pours the coffee from a height, with the ease of someone who has done this ten thousand times.

The ritual over, our tongues relax in praise of the coffee divine. Stored heat rises from our naked arms and damp shirt backs, and when the children crowd in to show us their handiwork the kitchen becomes the centre of a party that none of us want to leave. This is our first mid-morning coffee, our first opportunity to talk about the farm with a bit of its soil under our nails. We drink slowly, and it's only when the children have shown every one of us their favourite handmade Pokémon card and returned to their makeshift factory that we leave this sanctuary to pick the last of today's offerings.

~

In only a few days we've become part of *Il Granello*'s rhythm. This might be what it's like to live in a commune. I like it.

Romano is whistling again, the same old infectious tune. We've all found something to pick or pull in rows within earshot of the melody. I'm laying down a humming track, Henry is laying down the words and Patti is backing up the chorus. Shannon doesn't sing as a rule, but I can see him keeping time in the dig-twist-pull of each weed extraction. *Don't worry, I'm happy*. I feel the doubts that crept in when we were in Calabria receding. Right now, we're doing exactly what we have been dreaming of, and it feels just right.

At lunch we all find a place at the garden table. Elisa and Romano are fluent in English, but their children speak almost none. They turn to Henry for words they can use with our boys, and Riley has learned to do the same (Aidan relies heavily on pantomime). When they've all eaten their fill they disappear into the garden shed and reappear a few minutes later with the litter of kittens. Pouncing on the bright spots of sunlight playing across the lawn, the kittens lead the children in an erratic dance.

Coffee marks the end of lunch, but not the start of work. On day one, Elisa told us they never work in the heat of the day. 'It is a time to rest,' she said.

'If you like, you can go for a walk around the escarpment, or into the village. Or, like me, you can have a sleep.' Elisa collects the empty glasses then catches my eye. 'The children, I think, are now friends. They will be happy to play together.' Her smile is one of relief.

'Repose?' I suggest to Shannon. We leave the children to the kittens and each other and retreat to our room.

Once the heat of the day has waned, we head to the herb room on the top floor of the house. Herbs hang in bunches from the ceiling like a colony of bats. Others are loosely spread over the surface of fine mesh screens resting on trestles. The air in this room is heavily aromatic and intoxicating, and I think for a moment that I'm still in an afternoon doze.

'This is how we started,' Elisa says, running her fingers through tiny yellow orbs of camomile. The smell stirs a memory of babies and sleepless nights. 'But it did not work as we hoped.' She reaches up to unhook a bouquet of dried oregano, the colony shivers as one, then settles as she removes her hand and her catch.

'Dried herbs are not essential, so it was hard to get people to even stop at our stall,' she says.

'So, what did you do?' I ask.

'We noticed that when we took a few vegetables, just excess from our garden, people would stop to buy them, and sometimes they would purchase a herb salt or a dried bunch, but usually they just wanted the vegetables. So we started to grow more. It was hard, because we had planted so many rows of *basilica* and *timo* and *cipollina* and *salvia* ...' the words stop but her head keeps nodding indicating a long list. 'We had to dig them up to plant zucchini and *pomodoro*.'

'Trial and error,' I say, wondering briefly about how Shannon and I would cope with failure.

'Yes. I miss the aromatics, I would like to work more with them, but it is not what people want and we need to make money, so now most of our efforts are for vegetables.'

'But you still have a lot of herbs. You must enjoy escaping up here in the afternoon?' I say.

'We still take them to the markets, but not so much. At holiday times they sell better. People buy the salts and packaged herbs as gifts. We are even experimenting with drying vegetables.'

Elisa motions us over to a chest of drawers. It stands almost as tall as me and as wide as a piano. When she slides out one of the drawers I see that the base has been replaced with more fine mesh. Spread across it are hundreds of pale-green discs.

'Zucchini,' she tells us. 'We always have too much in summer, and they don't keep, so they end up in Pancetta's bucket and make us no money at all.'

Shannon and I laugh. We have our own love–hate relationship with zucchini. It grows in such abundance in our garden, and with so little attention, that for three months of each year it appears in almost every meal. We're developing an intense hatred of it but can't relinquish the easy success or the undeserved pride of seeing it thriving in our vegetable patch.

'So what will you do with it all?' Shannon asks. I can tell he's going to put the answer away for safe keeping.

'Package it up and sell it as an ingredient for soup when the weather cools and there are no fresh zucchini at the markets.'

'That's a brilliant idea,' I say.

Shannon wants to know how the drier works, and the absurd flame in the fireplace downstairs is explained.

'We capture heat from the flu and direct it into the bottom of the drawers. We have to keep the fire going very low all summer if we are drying this much food. As long as we keep the doors and windows open, we don't really notice.'

I help Elisa to choose herbs for the afternoon market in Bologna then we all meet at the front of the house to pack the car with baskets of produce. Today she'll take Patti to help, it's her last night and this will be her last chore as a WWOOFer. As much as I'd like to join them, only two people can fit in the Subaru with all the vegetables. I spend the rest of the afternoon slicing zucchini for the drier, while Shannon works in the field with Romano and Henry.

When we sit down for dinner I'm tired and aching, but my mind is calm. The vegetables sold well at the market, and Elisa can barely keep her eyes open. A relaxed smile plays across her face like the sunlight played across the lawn just hours ago. It's a moment of clarity for me after weeks of ambivalence – they live a happy life, and a good one, by toiling for something real.

~

It's Saturday. Our working day has ended with another long lunch and now we're driving in a convoy of two through the hills surrounding Bologna. The quiet road winds and climbs, then a few cars come into view, then a few more. They're parked precariously anywhere there's space. We pull in behind the last car and spill out of our vehicles, each of us carrying a contribution to this evening's feast.

Our shadows are long when we arrive on the hill, but it's high and should catch another hour or so of sunlight. Twenty people stand on their left legs, their right feet against their inner thighs and their hands in prayer above their heads. Tree pose, it's called. They're a colourful contrast against the blue sky. Elisa, Romano and Henry immediately join their ranks. The children – all five – join a crowd of youngsters chasing each other on the grassy slopes. Neither Shannon nor I are confident we can maintain our balance on one leg so we find a place to watch from the sidelines.

When a young woman in Indian print approaches us I'm reminded of being at a show at the Adelaide Fringe and praying not to be asked to go on stage. She's carrying two flimsy yoga mats, which she offers to us with some friendly Italian banter. Shannon's reply gives our origins away and the conversation proceeds in English.

'Please, join in. The poses are gentle so you do not need to know yoga. You are very welcome,' she says, putting the mats in our arms.

We smile, as if this invitation was exactly what we'd been waiting for, then walk reluctantly to the middle of the hill and raise our hands in prayer.

From a distance, these hills are the rolling green of poetry. On our way here I imagined strolling barefoot up the gentle slope then lying back upon the cushion of soft grass to daydream in the fading light. On closer inspection, I realise that the green grass sprouts from the pale rigid carcasses of last season. It's like armour around the new growth – effective armour. I struggle to hold my one-legged pose, and when I lurch to the right I'm forced to save myself by planting my foot on solid ground. I should have prayed for balance and a thicker mat. The thin veneer between me and the earth is no barrier to the spear of grass that finds the ball of my foot. I grind my teeth – this is no place for expletives – and move my mat a few inches to the left.

The farce continues through triangle pose and warrior pose and downward dog. Each is interrupted by a little dance of pain and a repositioning of my disintegrating yoga mat – it has so many holes that it's beginning to look like it's been crocheted. When I look over at Shannon he's wobbly but his efforts are earnest.

We're told to lie on our backs with our knees bent. I position myself between spears and indulge in a full yogic breath, as instructed. The mountain air is calming. Disobediently, I keep my eyes open – there's nothing between me and the sky except for the occasional grasshopper. We all breathe in and out together, creating a pulsating hum as if we're all parts of the same organism. I notice Shannon has his eyes closed and that his face is slack. What unexpected bliss to be on this hill in Italy, moving and breathing as one with all these good people.

We transition into a shoulder stand – first our knees come slowly up towards our heads, then twenty-five pairs of legs rise into the air in unison. There is total silence. We're a congregation with our heads bowed.

But I've failed to factor in the slope, and suddenly my toes no longer point skyward. My legs won't stay vertical, they veer towards my face, still straight but headed for the ground. I haven't done a sit-up for ten years, and that night of belly dancing with Simona has done nothing to develop the muscle required to pull my legs back up. My shoulders lift from the ground (contrary to instruction) then the weight of my hips propels my whole body backwards. Instinctively I bend my knees and bring my arms in to protect my face from the spikey ground. I roll once, not quite like a gymnast, then twice, not quite like a three-year-old, then I do a kind of sideways flop that stops my descent down the hill but delivers a sprinkling of dirt to my open mouth.

I know I look ridiculous and a snort escapes me. It's the sound I make when I'm trying not to laugh on solemn occasions. I can't tell if it's my snorting or the duration of the pose, but legs start to waver and some collapse. We're separate organisms again.

Our instructor suggests corpse pose and a few minutes of meditation. Thank all the Hindu gods, I think.

It turns out I'm not the only one with puncture wounds and a rash from rolling in the grass. While we feast, we compare the damage done to our mats and laugh at the image of our earnest selves trying to overcome the grass and gravity. It's not what we expected, not what the organisers planned, but it was fun and it was shared and we will all go home happy.

~

I can't decide whether my favourite place on this farm is the herb room with its warm perfume, or this cool-room. I've just delivered my final basket of figs and am taking pleasure in the scent of groundwater steeped in stone, and the cool air generated by its evaporation – it's been another sweltering morning. The heat has sped up the ripening of the figs and so we've spent the hours between our morning coffee and lunch picking them. It's a delicate task, and each fruit needs the picker's full concentration if the stalk and the flesh are to remain intact. None of us managed this every time.

As I bit into another damaged fig Shannon whispered with a smile, 'Pip, you're literally eating into their profit.'

'I think of it more as quality control,' I replied.

I'm sated, in so many ways. Sweetness lingers on my lips, and the neatly stacked baskets filled with fresh organic food give me a serene sense of fulfilment. Over two hours we've filled four baskets with ripe fruit, stalks attached. We've worked together and in tune, and this afternoon our baskets of food will go to market. It's not so hard to imagine doing this in the Adelaide Hills. I wonder how long a fig tree takes to grow?

I meet Elisa in the kitchen. She and Alice are making pasta.

'*Grattini*,' Elisa says when I ask what it is. She's made pasta dough and Alice is pulling off tiny bits and rolling them into irregular balls not much larger than grains of rice.

'They're so small. It must take a while,' I say.

'Not so long,' she assures me.

My stomach growls at the thought of a delayed lunch, but then she joins Alice in picking off bits of pasta and invites me to do the same. I watch as one hand follows the other, swift and dextrous. The pasta is rolled between two fingers and dropped into a bowl. I do my best to mimic her technique, and the ball of dough reduces quickly. All the while Elisa talks, sometimes to me, sometimes to Alice. I can see Elisa as an eight-year-old girl, her eyes almost too large for her delicate head, looking to her own mother for confirmation and praise. There's no doubt she received it, and now she's passing it on.

I try to ask Alice what she enjoys most about growing food. So often it's the boys we say we want this life for, but I'm not convinced they care that much. I know for sure they would choose junk food over an apple pulled fresh from the tree.

Alice looks to her mum for translation, then back to her busy hands. She shrugs, not sure.

'It has been hardest for Alice,' says Elisa. 'She is very shy and does not always feel comfortable with strangers in the house.' She bends to kiss Alice on the top of her head and Alice looks up and smiles.

'But it must be great to be home all the time, the kids must love that.'

'Well, I'm not really home; I'm in the field or at the market. During the summer I have hardly any time to play or even help with homework.' She looks towards Alice with an expression of apology. 'We all look forward to the winter. When the ground is frozen we stop hosting WWOOFers and the children have us all to themselves.'

The grattini is served with fish and a tomato sauce. The tiny balls soak up the juices and the effort involved is rewarded with the silence of savouring and then a clamour of compliments. Elisa passes all gratitude on to Alice, who beams. When we've eaten far more than our fill, the children recruit Shannon to a game of *mosca cieca* or 'blind fly' – we know it as 'blind man's bluff'. Lorenzo puts a hood over Shannon's head and the bluffing begins. The children can barely contain their giggling to make the required calls. Shannon lurches at them, always missing, and always leaving squeals of delight in his wake. These drawn-out lunches are the summer routine at *Il Granello*, and I wonder if Elisa's concern about the time she spends with her children is misplaced.

'Would you like to help me at the market this evening?' Elisa asks me while we watch.

It's like being asked to the ball. 'Of course I'd like to help, I thought you'd never ask,' I say, and we both laugh.

When we lived in Sydney the organic market in Frenches Forest was our weekly dose of the good life. At first it was enough to just wander around with a cane basket and fill it with a bit of fruit and a loaf of bread; we went as much for the atmosphere as for the food. It was relaxed and colourful, and had none of the Saturday morning angst that met us when we walked through the sliding doors of Woolworths. But over a few years the market became a symbol of our growing dreams. The egg man would show us photos of his happy hens. The couple who sold bread would chat about how early they were up that morning, but reassure us of the pleasure brought by the smell of rising dough. The potato man always had dirt under his fingernails from digging up the spuds the evening before, and the mushroom man could never be persuaded to reveal the location of his gathering grounds. 'What a good way to live,' one of us would say, almost every time we got back in the car to drive home.

Today we're heading for an organic market that's held every Thursday in the parking lot of a school in Bologna. As we drive from the hills into the city, I can't help thinking about what Shannon and I might take to market in the not-too-distant future.

We get there around five in the afternoon, find our spot and start setting up the marquee. The black asphalt is unforgiving. There's no shade and no breeze, and the vegetables are sweating in the back of the car. By the time we've laid out the produce, we're exhausted. Then the first customers arrive and Elisa becomes animated and welcoming, as if she's just arrived at a party and hasn't been working since seven o'clock this morning.

Everything we've picked over the past few days is arranged neatly across two long tables. Zucchinis are the dominant theme. When I take a turn around the market, I realise Zucchinis are the dominant theme at all the vegetable stalls, and I wonder how ours will sell. Small queues are beginning to form, so I take my place next to Elisa and prepare to be useful.

It's harder than I thought it would be. My recent revision of Italian words for numbers and weights, vegetables and herbs, hasn't equipped me for the rapid-fire enquiry coming from a stylish middle-aged woman in a black suit. She's picked up a light-green, young and slender zucchini with the flower still attached; I remember picking it, and all its stablemates, just before Romano called us in for coffee this morning. But I have no idea what she's asking. Is it the price? I tell her – I think – and point to where it's written on the box just in case. She shakes her head, picks up another zucchini, the larger sort Shannon collected, and tries to explain herself with more words. I wonder if she can see my heart pounding in my chest, or smell the sweat that has just sprung from my armpits. Her words have disassembled into an alphabet soup, and all I can do is offer her an apologetic smile. It must come across as a grimace, because she suddenly leans back as if she's only just realised I'm unhinged. Elisa comes over and explains my disability. While she gathers a selection of zucchini, the market-goer engages me in a slower conversation, her broad smile encouraging me to try. But I understand very little, and the resulting pantomime is holding up the queue. I pass Elisa a paper bag for the zucchinis she's selected and my role is set. I become the bag lady, and customers throw me compassionate smiles but little conversation, for the best part of an hour.

When the early rush dies down I'm released to look around. I need something thirst-quenching, so I join the queue for the fruit stall. I use the waiting time to practise my request: *due pesce per favore*, two peaches please. My mouth is watering with the thought of them, and when I reach the counter I'm afraid my words will sound gargled.

'*Due pesce per favore*,' I say, perfectly. The response is a furrowed brow and a string of unfamiliar words, so I try a second time. Again I execute the line with perfection. This time the response is more widespread – words from behind me, words from beside me, more words and the hint of a grin from the young man who grows the big fat peaches. Third time lucky, I think, and I raise my voice in case volume was the problem all along.

'*Due pesce per favore*.'

Volume appears not to be the problem. Peach man is laughing, the queue is laughing.

Someone in the middle of the queue leans forward to explain the joke. 'The fishmonger is next door.'

'But I don't want fish, I want peaches,' I say.

'*Pesca*, you want *pesca* not *pesce*.'

I turn my flushed face to peach man, but before I can correct my request he's handing me a bag with three large peaches, for which he only accepts the price of two. Then I hear more words from my translator.

'He says, you sounded like an Italian when you asked for fish, so he just assumed you had the wrong stall.'

Something light and bright rises in my chest, and a small secret is revealed – I wish I was Italian. It's a childish thought, and reminds me of wishing I was Olivia Newton John when I was ten. It was never going to happen: my voice was weak and my hair was dark brown, and even before the chubbiness of adolescence set in, I couldn't have squeezed into the black, vacuum-sealed outfit she wore in *Grease*. Being Italian is equally out of reach, I know, but for just a moment a real Italian thought I was a local. I will hang on to this like a magic bean, and maybe, if I water it with Italian lessons and fertilise it with regular visits to Italy, staying with our new friends or, better still, in a beautiful old apartment in the centre of Lucca with nothing but window boxes to weed, maybe then I would actually become Italian …

The heat must be making me lightheaded and fanciful. I return to Elisa's stall and offer her a peach. She takes it, grateful – it's the only useful thing I've done since we arrived.

'You know, Pip, if you stayed with us for six months you would be speaking fluently, like Henry,' she says.

It would be as simple as that. But of course it wouldn't. I take a bite of my peach and release the sunshine caught beneath its skin. When I'm rehydrated and sticky with juice from chin to fingertips I do the sensible thing and store the image of an Italian me in a cupboard at the back of my mind.

~

Elisa is crying. I can hear her in the bedroom below ours, her soft sobbing interrupted by searching questions. Romano's gentle reassurance barely stems the flow of tears. Something about her life has overwhelmed her, made her fragile and uncertain – she's scared. These things sound the same in any language. Otherwise the house is quiet: all the children are asleep and Henry is far away in a room at the other end of the second-floor corridor. We can't help but listen.

Shannon and I don't speak, we're afraid our whispers will intrude. I've sobbed like this, and now I feel the anxiety of it like a wave in my belly. Since we arrived, the optimism of Romano's whistled anthem has been reinforced by the daily joy of working, eating and relaxing with him and Elisa, and watching our children become more and more attached to one another. The dream I've had of the good life sits companionably beside the reality of *Il Granello*, and I've come to believe in the possibility of living it. Their example interrupted my uncertainty and propelled me back, like a pendulum, towards a good life of my own.

But now, as Elisa's distress tires itself out, I hesitate. The satisfaction of a good market, of coming home with empty crates and a bag full of cash, is diluted by Elisa's tears. I realise that the takings from tonight would have been no more than a day's pay on the modest wage I had back home. At best, it would only come in three times a week, and they would have to deduct rent, bills and the cost of food for their family and at least four hungry WWOOFers.

I feel the pendulum lose momentum, just short of the goal. I know I could reach out into space and bridge the gap – grab hold of the good life, tears and all – but once again I'm filled with uncertainty. As I did with Lauren at *Pirapora*, I've overlooked some deeper experience at *Il Granello*. I've focused too much on my own reactions to living on these farms – the physical discomforts and the emotional rewards. I haven't recognised them as temporary, impossible to compare to the difficult and sustained routine of these women's lives. I'm not sure I have either Lauren's or Elisa's virtues – their determination, resilience and strength of will. And there's not much evidence that they suffer my weakness for sleeping in or my lifelong habit of putting off until tomorrow that which I could, in all honesty, if I wasn't so lazy, do today.

I should talk to Shannon, but saying any of this out loud will give it substance and make it much harder to get rid of when I change my mind in the morning. And anyway, to say anything now would only disturb the delicate quiet that has finally come to rest on Elisa. It's like a thin frost on the tender growth of spring, and shouldn't be disturbed by anything other than sunshine.

~

The sun has risen, and I look at Elisa from under the brim of my hat. There's no sign of last night's turmoil. Romano, as usual, is whistling 'Don't Worry, Be Happy', but now I hear it differently. It's a secret message. It's not for us wwooFers; it's for Elisa. She is, as always, the only one not singing along, but she's stopped her picking and is smiling at him across the rows of vegetables. There's no sadness in her eyes. Instead, it's as if she's woken up to find herself exactly where she wants to be.

In the afternoon, Shannon builds Romano and Elisa a compost bay and fills it with waste – it's his farewell gift. Every day at *Il Granello*, wwooFers pull out piles of weeds and grass that could be mixed with manure from the pony and soiled straw from the chicken barn to produce a rich, loamy compost that will help the vegetables to grow. It's the staple of our garden at home and is curiously absent here. Romano is enthusiastic, and the two of them spend the afternoon working out the most efficient way to get weeds to the compost bay, and compost to the fields.

They talk a lot, often in Italian, each as enthusiastic as the other. From where I stand I can see the passion they have for what they're doing, and their abiding belief in its worth. I can also see joy. They're caught up, not just in this moment but the future it offers – some utopia where weeds don't dominate and tomatoes grow faster. A smile erupts across my face. Shannon has just stuck a garden fork into the compost pile like a mountaineer sticks a flag in Everest. He's claiming it, and I think he knows that it represents something that defines him.

What would I stick a flag in, I wonder? I'd like to think a well-made loaf, but it's just as likely to be a glass of red wine on a table facing a cluttered street, in an ancient city where fragments of an aria or the notes of a trumpet can settle like seeds in my imagination. I shake the thought from my head: the two images are uncomfortably incompatible.

'Coffee's on,' I call as I walk towards them.

They finish their conversation. Shannon laughs, Romano laughs. He puts his hand on Shannon's shoulder and says one more thing before switching to English.

'Coffee. Wonderful,' he says. 'Shannon is teaching me good things about compost. It will improve our systems, and this pleases me very much.'

Later, when the house is quiet and we've gone to bed, I lie awake. I'm thinking of Shannon and Romano, their shared labour and parallel dreams. Right now I want to stay and see how it all turns out, to learn Italian, to become close to Elisa and Romano and watch our children grow up together.

'Every now and then I think about an alternative life,' I whisper into the dark.

There's no answer, but I know he's awake.

'Shan?'

'What kind of alternative life?' He sounds wary, and suddenly I'm not sure what I was going to say.

~

In just two weeks we've become woven into the fabric of *Il Granello*. Pulling ourselves out of it leaves us feeling unravelled. Lorenzo and Alice offer the boys a pile of handmade Pokémon cards. In return they're given cards brought from home and printed in English. They all embrace, like cousins would after one of their regular visits. But our children may never visit again. From Riley's and Lorenzo's expressions I guess that they know this. Despite their shy natures and the barriers of language, they recognised each other and immediately felt comfortable. In two weeks they've forged bonds that would normally take months or even years.

It feels like this for all of us. We each have our own what-if scenarios – what-if we just cancelled the next farm and stayed here for another few weeks? What-if we moved here for a year, or indefinitely? What-if we jumped right off the deep end and committed to this good life with these good people in this good place?

That's where it all comes unstuck. This isn't our place. Our place lies fallow, overrun with grass grown thick and tall on winter rain. Our place is waiting for a commitment of some kind, and that's the reason we're here. We won't have the luxury of just contributing to something good while others do all the worrying.

Another what-if, barely audible in the way of uncomfortable truths – what-if I can't commit? What-if my good life is no longer the good life Shannon dreams about? What-if?

Elisa drives us to the bus stop and waits with us for the bus. Our conversation is stilted now. Only a few words are robust enough for final partings: sorry, thank you, I love you. When the time comes, I choose all three. I hear the laboured motor of the bus and turn to Elisa. Our faces, like our sons', reflect each other. She comes close and wraps her long arms around me.

'The children are sad to see you go,' she says.

'And we're sorry to go,' I reply. 'If we'd known we were going to fall in love with you all we would have organised to stay for months.'

We separate but hang on to each other's hands. 'Thank you, Elisa, for all your kindness.'

Her large eyes shine, she nods and lets me go. Then she embraces Shannon and the boys with the same affection.

When the bus pulls up we're all strangely quiet and reflective, you'd never know we were on our way to Venice for a few days' holiday before the next farm. Shannon and I gather our packs, and I overhear Elisa telling Aidan that Henry tried to feed Pancetta her breakfast this morning and Pancetta charged at him.

'She wanted you to do it, and blames Henry for you leaving,' she says.

Aidan and Pancetta bonded over that morning ritual of the scrap bucket, and his face lights up. Elisa coaxed the same smile out of him on the day we arrived, and here it is at our departure – they're perfect bookends to our time at *Il Granello*.

Venice

(Throw your map away)

It's all the potential in a visit to Venice that makes the experience disappointing. I know this as soon as I'm standing on the concourse outside the *Stazione di Venezia Santa Lucia*, looking at the church of *San Simeon Piccolo*. It's a misnomer – the church is not small. Wide steps meet Greek columns that are topped by an impressive green dome. It's twice the height of the four-storey buildings surrounding it. Between the church and me is the Grand Canal, a wide ribbon almost exactly the same colour as the church's dome, and on it a flotilla of gondolas. My eyes can't open wide enough … but then I notice the crowds weighing down the wharf that floats on the canal, and the queues for the *vaporetto*. Young children are crying from heat and the fatigue of travel, and their parents look desperate. Elderly couples stand close together scrutinising guidebooks, maps, printed instructions from hotels. Only the backpackers look comfortable in this throng – they've done this in every city across Europe.

I look around for the lovers. Venice should be their mecca but they are nowhere to be seen. No one whispers in their companion's ear, allowing their lips to brush the lobe, their tongue to stray. There's no kissing, no careless stroking. Maybe this isn't the season for making love in Venice – it's too hot, too humid, and far too crowded. I realise my first disappointment and am glad for it; the conditions couldn't be better for a visit with children in tow, and I no longer regret our miserly booking of a single room.

We're the last onto the *vaporetto*, which gives us the best position. The railing comes down behind us and we swivel to lean on it, delighted that we can turn our backs on the crowd in the boat and instead watch Venice reveal herself. We coast along the serpentine length of one of the world's most famous canals, struck by the impossible beauty of it all. Palaces glide by, towers and more domes. We pass a fresh food market, and exclamations from the crowd behind herald the Rialto Bridge. I'm speechless, a rare thing, but there's no time to comment on one sight before another demands attention. What the locals must take for granted – the houses that shelter them, the gondolas they travel in, the bridges they walk over to get from home to school to work to friends – in me creates a yearning, the sour taste of envy and a discontent for the place I call home. Who deserves to live here, and what can I do to be one of them? By the time we're delivered to *Piazza San Marco* I'm delirious.

'It's the heat,' Shannon says when I say I feel faint. He insists I sit down before we attempt to navigate the tight laneways in search of our hotel. It's a mistake.

We only have two days here, and time is already running out. It's like arriving at the buffet breakfast of a fancy hotel fifteen minutes before it closes. I'm paralysed with the fear of choosing the wrong sights and leaving this city dissatisfied.

Twenty-five years ago, en route to Switzerland, my train pulled into *Stazione di Venezia Santa Lucia*. The guard announced that the onward journey would be delayed by twenty minutes, so I took the opportunity to stretch my legs. There were no crowds that day, and my eighteen-year-old eyes had never seen anything like it. Not in a guidebook – I didn't have one. Not on the internet – it didn't exist. Not in the photograph albums of friends – I was the first to escape my childhood home. I'd heard of Venice, of course. I'd probably seen something about it on television, but it was in the same category as Disneyland. It was hardly real.

I fill my lungs with the hot, humid air of Venice and let my eyes close. I'm aware of my swollen feet and the slackened skin on the backs of my hands, but nothing else betrays the years that have passed since I was last in Italy. Memories that have been dormant for decades flutter against my eyelids. The smell of this place, the sight of the canal and the sound of foreign voices – I'm eighteen again, and I've come to Italy to be inspired. I want to be a fashion designer.

A fashion designer! Really? The thought is comic and disturbing. My eyes pop open and I look down at my clothes: an ill-fitting T-shirt and ankle-length op-shop skirt, which was never worn by someone with taste, but which I thought might lend me the romantic appearance of an alluring earth-mother while I floated along rows of tomatoes, picking only the ripest and holding them to my nose to inhale their organic scent. Of course, such attire is completely impractical, and this became obvious when I trudged amongst the raspberry canes at *Il Mulino*. Stinging nettle kept catching in the swish of my hem, and my legs became mottled and itchy. There was nothing alluring about it. Since then I've worn a pair of elasticated cargo pants and a pink long-sleeved shirt whenever I'm out in the fields. I've also avoided all mirrors and reflective glass.

But I did once dream of being a fashion designer, and I'm trying to think when that dream was forgotten.

I stood on the wharf that day, between the station and the Grand Canal, and burst into tears. There was only one traveller's cheque left in my wallet – emergency money to get me to relatives in the UK if the nanny job in Switzerland didn't work out. I had enough change to buy a packet of dry biscuits and a bottle of water. I wished desperately that I'd stayed on the train and spared myself the knowledge of what I was missing. I promised myself I'd come back. Perhaps in a few months, after I'd earned some money. I'd make Italy my home and Venice would be in my back yard. All I needed was a well-paying job, and surely that was guaranteed – I had a glowing reference from my Year Twelve Textiles and Design teacher, and four weeks' work experience as a barmaid in Greece.

The nanny job in Switzerland didn't last long, and within a month I was working in a nursing home in Slough, England, spooning mush into speechless mouths and wiping bums. It didn't pay well, and a year after I'd left, I was back in Australia. Venice didn't even make it into my photo album; I'd run out of film.

So here I sit, in the shadow cast by the *Basilica di San Marco*, holding back complicated emotions brought on by the sudden realisation that I never made Italy my home. That the life I'd looked forward to throughout my adolescence had evaporated without me noticing. It's taken me twenty-five years and another dream to get back to Venice, and again time threatens to tear me away too soon. The guidebook doesn't help – unlike in Lucca, there are at least seventy must-do sights and activities. I'm standing in front of my metaphorical buffet, starving, but unable to choose.

Then I remember a little gem of a book I found in a pile of discards at my local library. *Venice is a Fish* is a kind of guidebook, though it fails to mention almost every significant sight and lacks the detail that would help you locate a good hotel or the cheapest pizza. It's written by a Venetian, Tiziano Scarpa, and he takes you on a sensual tour of his beloved city. 'Throw your map away!' he writes. 'Why do you so desperately need to know where you are?'

Good question, I think. Though I don't have an answer. For now, I decide we should dawdle, as he suggests. Lose ourselves and drift on the tide of sensation.

~

I'm sitting on my pack in the middle of *Piazza San Marco*, agog at the Basilica. It's exotic and opulent, topped with delicate spires that look like candles on a cake, and iced in gold and coloured candy. But this isn't what's caught my eye. On a balcony, below gilded arches, is a group of novice priests. I can see them clearly through the viewfinder of my camera. Their faces are smooth and hairless, their bodies lean. I count eight, each in a long black cassock tapered into a slender waist and falling straight, over narrow hips, to the ground. Bands of virgin white encircle their necks and wrists – forcing poise, or just accentuating it. They're elegant and beautiful, and not all beyond vanity – some have allowed their regulation short hair to grow long at the front, quiffed and held in place. These same young men (I'm suddenly seeing beyond the black robes) wear sunglasses, more stylish than necessary.

I've stared long enough. I take a photograph of the young priests as they take their own photographs from the balcony. I wonder what images their cameras will hold. Perhaps, on closer inspection, they'll spot me in the crowd – a small, untidy figure, sitting on a backpack near the edge of the square, her camera tilted up.

I've caught my breath and tamed my thoughts. I wrestle my pack onto my back and follow Shannon's lead past the Basilica and into a congested lane coming off the square. We're looking for *Scala Contarini del Bovolo*, a small 15th-century palace with an extraordinary external spiral staircase. The name refers to a snail's shell, and if we find it we find our hotel. But navigating the narrow alleyways beyond *Piazza San Marco* is harder than we thought. Our packs aren't welcome, they knock and obstruct and irritate all those people wishing they'd chosen May or October for their romantic getaway. To make things worse, I'm terrified of losing Riley to the labyrinth, and a vision of his small, quiet self being bumped into a canal by the oblivious girth of a large American has glued my hand to his. There's an exaggerated sigh every time another pair must de-couple to slip past us.

Shannon stops and consults the map that I've agreed we can look at until we find the hotel. He's none the wiser. We retrace our steps. Carnevale isn't until February, but the masks and costumes that have made it famous adorn window display after window display. At another juncture, another wrong turn, the boys and I pick our favourite disguises while Shannon tries to solve the puzzle of the *calli*.

Aidan settles on a long-beaked bird with startled eyes. Riley chooses a pirate's costume. I'm tossing up between a fine-featured white porcelain face that could only be worn with the matching Marie Antoinette dress, and a more honest mask depicting joy on one side, sorrow on the other. There's something unsettling about it. My face is reflected in the glass and superimposed, and I feel like a fortune teller has just told me my fate.

'Follow me,' Shannon says. 'I think it's just around the corner.'

Our Venetian sanctuary has been decorated by its octogenarian owner and is a flouncy mishmash of bedspreads and cushions – I fall instantly in love, and realise I would never have made it in the fashion industry. But it's Riley who discovers the most extraordinary delight of our accommodation.

'Mum, Dad, look what I can see!'

He's sitting on the toilet – seat down, pants up – with the window beside him wide open. It's a front-row seat to Venice.

We take turns to sit and look down on the narrow canal. There's no footpath beneath our window, or on the other side. Stone foundations are sunk into the water and built on with the same ancient bricks that form the spiral staircase of the neighbouring palace. Small windows, just a metre above the waterline, have been bricked up against the *acqua alta*, or high water, of autumn. The walls above are rendered and crumbling, discoloured with age and mould. An oleander, full with pink and white flowers, reaches around the corner from some unseen courtyard. It's a picture of decrepit beauty, and we can view it, undisturbed by the rabble, at the most ordinary moments of our day.

I usher everyone out of the bathroom and turn on the water for a shower.

As I dry myself off I hear him. Until now, our little canal has been silent, despite the season and the crowds, which can only be explained by the buffer of closely built stone structures and the meandering habit of the waterways. He's a tenor, and his song is slow and rhythmic, as if the tempo is being set by the drop-push-lift of his oar. When he takes a breath I listen for the approach of the gondola, but hear nothing. It's a stealthy craft, and I think of how useful that would have been for Casanova.

The song resumes and the gondola glides beneath the bathroom window. It has passengers, a family of four that are willing and able to fork out eighty euros for a half-hour ride. If any of them looks up they'll see me. But people rarely look up, so I stand here, my wet body wrapped in a towel, listening to the gondolier sing to them. The gentle song laps against my ears, even after they've passed under the oleander and out of sight.

Energy restored, we venture back out, past our spiral sentry and into the slipstream of people heading away from *Piazza San Marco*. We've left the map behind and are following our senses. The boys want to stop at the first *pasticceria*, but Shannon and I decide to search for something in a quieter location.

The *calle* opens into a campo – it would be called a piazza in any other part of Italy, but in Venice there's only one piazza and it belongs to *San Marco*. The white noise fades. Then a real sound, clear and singular, stretches towards us. A bow is being drawn across the strings of a violin. It orients us, and we move towards it, even though the boys protest – there's no *pasticceria* that they can see. I reassure them that there'll be one just around the corner, because there always is.

The violinist sports an out-of-shape white fedora. He has an old face, darkly tanned, deeply lined, and framed by grey hair. When he looks up his eyes are unusually blue.

We scuttle past, the boys intent on seeing what the next corner will reveal. It's a gelateria. Aidan asks if they have Pokémon flavour – his hopeful habit has followed us since Rome. The woman holding the scoop clearly has no idea what he's talking about, so without a second thought Aidan selects *fragola* and *stracciatella*, strawberry and choc-chip. When we each have a cup piled high with our favourite flavours, we return to the violinist. The boys are compliant now, so we find a stretch of pavement shaded by a stone wall and sit between splodges of chewing gum.

The old man is accomplished, as far as I can tell. I'm not usually a fan of the violin. Having endured it during countless school concerts, I've usually found it high-pitched and whiney. But now, in this impossible place, it makes the most beautiful music. The instrument is as old as its player, scarred all over, and where the varnish has peeled the wood has lost its honey tone and become grey.

No one else stops, no one applauds. I want to stay until the last curtain call. I wonder how often he comes out to play, how much he earns and whether this is a joy or a terrible indignity. I wonder if he's Venetian or a refugee, another desperate person earning money as best he can.

When we were lost this morning between *San Marco* and our hotel we heard the whizz of flying toys. A young man was releasing them into the air, fishing for the attention of the boys, getting it, and cajoling us to buy one. We refused. Then we heard a shout from another man with the same dark skin, in a language I thought might be Ethiopian. Not that I know what Ethiopian sounds like, but their faces made me think of the famine that ravaged that country and the constant television coverage that once got me thinking that aid work could be a good alternative to fashion – it was a time of fickle dreams. The salesman's grin disappeared as he hastily packed up his merchandise. He ran with his friend into the crowd, the sound of their footfall heavy and fast. It was a complete contrast to the browsing slowness of the rest of us, with our visas stamped clearly in our passports, and our experience of famine nothing more than a few unforgettable images and a song we all bought each other for Christmas in 1984. The young men vanished, and a few seconds later two *polizia* walked past the place where the whizzing toys had been displayed.

'Please can we get one?' Riley asked. But by then it was as if they'd never been there at all.

There is no whizzing of cheap toys now, just the sweet sound of the violin. We stay listening until our gelato cups have all been licked clean by Aidan. I give the boys two euros each to place in the violin case and wonder briefly how fashion and humanitarianism could have coexisted in my adolescent mind. Then we walk away.

Shannon goes in search of bottled water and I sit with the boys on the stairs of a small bridge that joins the campo to another tangle of lanes. There's nothing purely utilitarian in this city. Below the hand rail of this bridge, wrought iron has been fashioned into an intricate design of curves and curls. If I hadn't sat on its steps I wouldn't have noticed. Through them I can see Venice reflected in the glassy green of the canal. The buildings that rise out of it have shimmering twins, with their own shimmering decay and their own shimmering sky. Black iron twists itself around a submerged balcony, trying to hold its fluid form. I search for the Venetian who might live there, and a woman floats out. She has my face, and her feet are webbed.

'This place stinks!'

I can always count on Aidan to bring me back to earth. I hadn't noticed, but he's right – this place does stink. Mostly, it's like the stems of flowers that have been in a vase for too long. And there's the faint smell of sewage.

Shannon returns with water – and panini.

'I'm not eating lunch in a toilet,' Aidan says. He rises from his stair, but contradicts himself immediately by taking a bite of the roll.

'Need a hand?' Shannon is offering his. It's cool from holding the bottle of water, so I transfer it to my cheek and close my eyes. Then I look back through the fretwork of the bridge to the empty balcony. If I wanted, I could reach through the curling bars and dip my fingers in the canal, puncture the glassy green. It's tempting, but something beautiful would be disturbed. I let myself be pulled to standing.

We didn't plan to return to the *Piazza San Marco*, but we float on the current of the crowd and end up there anyway. We pass Café Florian, and I reach in through an open window to run my fingertips along the back of a chair covered in red velvet. It's surprisingly cool, and I have a sudden urge to feel it against the backs of my knees and to rest my head against the cold marble tabletop while I wait for someone to bring me a drink on a silver tray. But an orange juice costs eleven euros, so I withdraw my hand and ask Shannon to pass me our water – it's lost all its chill.

It's inevitable that we join the queue to enter the Church of Gold. But the sun blinds and burns us, so I suggest that Shannon sit with the boys in the nearby shadows while I wait in line. Each second is a pulse in my chest. I'm conscious of time passing, conscious that two days may not be enough to see beauty beyond the crowds of Venice, conscious that when we leave here we'll be going to our last farm, and after that, we'll be going home. I'm starting to feel anxious that I won't find what I came looking for in Italy. It's like I've been shopping all day and there's only one store left open; if it doesn't have what I want I'll go home with sore feet and nothing to show for it.

'You look like you need to sit down,' says Shannon.

He takes my place in the line-up and I retreat with the boys to the covered walkway around the Doge's Palace.

When Shannon is finally at the head of the queue we race over to join him. We're waved into the Basilica and the crowds fall away. The first delight is a reviving drop in temperature, then the splendour of a gilded sky, a coloured floor that gives the impression of a hundred Persian rugs scattered thoughtlessly, and a jewel-encrusted golden alter piece. I touch everything I am allowed to touch and some things I'm not.

~

Our first day has meandered and exhausted itself. When the sun falls below the rooftops we find ourselves in *Campo Santa Margherita* with a distinctly younger crowd. They spill from bars around the square, gesticulating and speaking Italian. They've been sensibly indoors all day and have now come out to play.

'That place has the longest queue,' Shannon says. 'It must have the best pizza.'

The place he's pointing to, *Pizza Al Volo*, looks neglected. *Fuck the police* is scrawled across its concrete facade and the entrance is flanked by large bins dressed in torn black plastic liners. But there's no arguing with a queue of young Italians, so Shannon joins them. I go to the bar nearby and order two glasses of what everyone else is drinking.

'Spritz,' the man behind the bar shouts at me when I ask what it is. I watch him mix Prosecco with Aperol and a slice of orange. The plastic cups are disappointing. We've spent the afternoon coveting this rosy drink, watching it being sipped from bulbous glasses that catch the light and sparkle. As the day drained us, it started to look more like an elixir of life than a mere aperitif, something worthy of a quest.

I take ours back to the bench where the boys are waiting. They each have a slice of pizza that requires two hands to hold.

'This is the best pizza ever,' Aidan says, tomato sauce extending his already enormous smile.

Riley just nods, too preoccupied with eating to stop for conversation. I pass Shannon his spritz and raise mine in celebration. The cups don't clink, but in this place, with a large cardboard pizza box on my lap and the boys beside me with tomato sauce all over their faces, the slightly sweet fizz of the spritz couldn't taste better.

The sky darkens to sapphire and the heat subsides. People are starting to get drunk in *Campo Santa Margherita*. A man and woman lurch from side to side, talking too loudly. When he falls over a rubbish bin, she screeches at him, as if he's drawn unnecessary attention to them, as if she hasn't. They're ugly, but interesting, so we watch until he rights himself and they lurch towards us.

'Time for gelato, boys,' Shannon says. They're quick to respond.

We choose a *calle* at random. There's a footpath on both sides of this canal, with small flat motorboats tied parallel to their railings, the way cars would be parked in any other city on the planet. It's a residential street, and we're unexpectedly alone. This is when the imagination ranges through the possible and impossible. I fall into step with Shannon and hug his arm to my chest.

'Do you think we could live here?' I ask.

'Not really,' he says, without pausing to think.

He doesn't want to play along, and I feel a quickening in my chest. Shannon and I have set out on a journey together, with the same destination in mind, but I keep getting lost. Shannon knows exactly where he is in the scheme of his life, and he imagines himself in no other place. We walk in silence for a few minutes, and when an old man comes towards us leading an old dog, we separate.

The boys run ahead, stopping at tiny bridges to await our directions. I'm comfortably oblivious to where we are, and happy to cross a bridge simply to admire the filigree of its railing or to follow the curve of a *calle* beyond. For a while, Shannon follows my lead but when the last light of day has gone he calls me back.

'This way, Pip.'

I'm on the first step of a bridge that arches like a cat over the narrow canal we've been walking along. The boys are already halfway across, but they don't hesitate to turn back. They don't care which way we go, they just want to keep moving. As he passes, Riley takes my hand. I take a last look at a balcony spilling with flowers on the other side of the canal, then turn to catch up with Shannon.

He's operating without a map, but Shannon still seems to know where we are. Within ten minutes we're back on familiar ground. Even if I hadn't spied it on our arrival I would recognise the Rialto Bridge. It spans the Grand Canal like a tiara, the flash of cameras are its glittering jewels. Aidan and Riley sit on the water's edge, looking through a forest of timber poles sunk deep to stop the gondolas from straying. The hustle and bustle of the day is over, and the gondolas are resting. Some have had sheets of blue canvas thrown over them, others are open to the cloudless night. They're like horses freed from their saddles, fed and tethered. They nuzzle and clink and constantly shift their weight as the canal moves beneath them.

We could be in any time: there are no cars, no fumes, no advertising for Coca-Cola. People have retreated to the restaurants and theatres, and although we can hear them talking, we can't see the modern cut of their clothes or their mobile phones. In the dim light cast by old-fashioned street lamps, the only person we can see is wearing black trousers and a blue-and-white striped shirt – he's mooring his gondola. It's the Venice I'd hoped for and I want to capture it, but in doing so I cut it short: my camera is digital, and the flash is too bright.

～

Venice is beautifully impossible. Over the past two days we've been hot and bothered and short of time. The queues have been long, and the gondolas too expensive, but we forgive all these flaws because of all the beauty. Already we're gilding our memories of this city.

An hour before we're due to leave we're standing on the Bridge of Sighs. While we wait our turn to look at the view, Riley wants to know if we can come back one day and stay in the same hotel.

'I guess we can. Why do you like it so much?' I ask.

'I like the man who sings from his gondola right below the toilet. That wouldn't happen anywhere else.'

'What about you, Aidan, what do you love about Venice?'

'The pizza. They have the best pizza,' he says.

I've glimpsed so much and imagined much more. Last night, after the boys fell asleep, Shannon and I hatched a plan to return for a month, just as winter is turning to spring and before the crowds arrive. The year is yet to be determined, but the thought that it might happen is enough to soften the inevitable disappointment of leaving.

The tourists in front of us have moved on and it is our turn to look upon Venice one last time.

I stood in Venice, on the Bridge of Sighs;
A palace and a prison on each hand.

A name like this could only have been given by a poet, and once Byron had named it, the dream wrote itself. For nearly two hundred years people have imagined prisoners being taken from the interrogation rooms of the Doge's palace to the prison for execution. As they walked across this bridge, high and enclosed above the *Rio di Palazzo*, they would sigh at their last view of their beloved city.

But this isn't what really happened. Prisoners didn't walk across this bridge before going to their deaths – executions had ceased before it was even built. They didn't pause at the windows and take a last look – the view is obscured by a thick limestone lattice and, like us, they would have strained to see it. So what made Byron's alter ego sigh? What makes me?

In Venice Tasso's echoes are no more,
And silent rows the songless gondolier;
Her palaces are crumbling to the shore,
And music meets not always now the ear;
Those days are gone – but Beauty still is here.

As I stand between the Doge's palace and his prison, the life Shannon and I are seeking looms on both sides, and I realise that the dream I brought to Italy is crumbling, as other dreams of mine have crumbled. This time though, it's not just my dream, and the wave of nausea that comes over me isn't teenage regret: it's dread.

I'm afraid I want to turn away from our plans for a good life. I'm afraid that perhaps this whole idea was just something I borrowed from Shannon when love and babies, then study and work, crowded out all my thoughts of travel or fashion or doing good. Shannon spoke his dreams out loud, and images of the life he wanted fell on fertile ground – for years they grew well in me. But now? I'm not sure.

There are times when Venice floods, and times when she stinks, and times when she's so repressively hot and crowded that I've wanted to escape. But there are also times when I've seen her with a poet's eye and she's the Venice of my dreams, the beautiful impossible city, and I've wished I could stay forever.

My fingers are curled around the cool lattice separating me from a clear view. I know there's still beauty in the life we've been searching for, but I don't know if it's enough to hold me.

Piedmont

*(Look after your nails and don't be afraid
to paint them pink)*

Bells ring constantly in Venice, and eventually we stopped hearing them. But on our last night I was woken at midnight by the sonorous tone of the *Marangona*, the only survivor of five original bells housed in the *campanile*, or bell tower, of *San Marco*. Historically, the *Marangona* was rung to herald the start of the working day, so I suppose it makes sense that I can hear it now – though I'm struggling to figure out how the sound could travel so clearly from Venice to Cessole, a small village in the north of Italy, not far from Turin.

Seven perfect notes call me out of sleep. When the last is nothing more than an echo in my mind I roll over and nestle into Shannon's back. He's warm and motionless, and I sink back down, into the glassy green. When I look at my feet, they're webbed, and I realise I can glide through the water with the stealth of a gondola. There's the balcony, all darkness behind wrought iron, a blue sky undulating below it. If I dive down I can go inside, but when I do there is nothing. *Marangona* rings again, once, and I gasp for breath. Twice, and I feel Shannon shift in my arms. I open my eyes and hear the lesser bells of a local church, their song drifting down the valley and through our bedroom window. The message is the same. It's time to wake up and work.

We groan and pull pillows over our heads to drown out the intrusion.

'I think some spiteful monk's rigged those bells to chime twice,' I suggest, as Shannon swings his legs to sit on the edge of the bed.

'Church bells with a snooze setting? It beats an alarm.'

How right he is. By the time the seventh note is sung we're wide awake, and thoughts of coffee have replaced our dreaming.

We have our own apartment. It's like a hotel room, with a double bed and two singles, a sparkling ensuite and a kitchenette. It's attached to the main house and looks across a paved courtyard to a barn that has been beautifully converted into a bed and breakfast called *Tenuta Antica*, Old Estate. It feels wrong to be pulling on work boots.

Mauro is in the kitchen, and he shows us where to find everything. As at *Il Granello*, there's a cupboard full of cereal for the WWOOFers, and of course we're welcome to help ourselves to biscuits. This is good news indeed. Our boys have recently begun to ask when we're going home, but biscuity breakfasts should sustain them for another few weeks.

Pia comes in wearing a T-shirt that's not long enough to cover her underpants. She's still rubbing sleep from her eyes, and I wonder if she's forgotten we're here.

'*Buongiorno*, good morning, how did you sleep?' She's cheerful and without an ounce of shyness. When the other WWOOFers file into the kitchen there's no sign that she feels she should be dressed otherwise. Pia picks up where Mauro left off, telling us where to find the yoghurt and the bread, that both are in the restaurant if we run out of them in the house. She apologises for the early start.

'It is so hot,' she says, 'so we've been starting at 7.30 for the past few weeks to avoid the heat of midday. At eleven we stop – you will hear the bells – and in the evening we work for two more hours.'

I notice that she's painted her long fingernails white. Yesterday, when she met us at the station, they were fuchsia pink. It was because of her fingernails, and her pretty sandals, and the cotton dress she wore to just above her knees, that we hung back for so long. When the car park had emptied of all likely candidates, and I began to panic that arrangements for this final farm might have fallen through, we approached her.

'Yes, of course, I am Maria Pia. It is so good to meet you,' she'd said.

A boy comes tearing into the kitchen in the manner of a Hot Wheels car that has just been released across a smooth surface. His volume is at maximum, and there's urgency in his rapid release of words. He comes to a sudden halt against his mother, wraps both arms around one of her naked thighs, and the volume decreases. Pia is the perfect counterpoise. She strokes his dark hair and speaks with a quiet, soothing rhythm. By the time his older brother comes through the door the argument that propelled him is over.

'This,' Pia says to us, 'is Daniele. He is four and can get very excited.'

The older boy's face is stormy. She puts her arm around him and whispers something that makes him smile. 'And this young man is Luca, he is ten.'

An older woman shuffles in, not because of any infirmity, but to keep her slippers on her feet. Mauro hands her a coffee, and Pia introduces her as Anna, her mother.

'She speaks no English, but she understands a lot. You can practice your Italian with her.'

Three other WWOOFers make breakfast around our induction. Cherie and Paul are a couple in their late twenties, from New Zealand and Australia respectively. They've been here for two months and will stay another. They're comfortable and familiar, and they make Nonna laugh. Nicky is a young woman from the US, on her summer break. She has all the characteristic enthusiasm and optimism of her nationality and youth, but her buoyant chatter seems to rub against Nonna, who removes herself to the back deck for a cigarette soon after Nicky arrives.

When everyone has had their fill of coffee and biscuits, Mauro leads us to the vines on the hill behind the house. The others have been coming here every morning for a week, and they quickly disappear into yesterday's row, each with a pair of grape-pruning scissors.

Mauro demonstrates what he wants us to do.

'Why do you need to cut off so much?' I ask. The ground is littered with juvenile bunches, dehydrated rejects left to bake in the sun.

'If there is more than one cluster on a vine the energy and nutrients are spread thinner, and there will not be as much sugar in the fruit. It is the sugar that will make good wine, and so we choose the best clusters and prune the rest.'

Snip. A poorly formed bunch drops to the ground, leaving a more fortunate pendulum of green orbs to sweeten. Mauro hands Shannon his sharp pruning scissors and, with an apology, offers me an ancient pair of secateurs. They're heavy, and the blades are large and round and black. They look like they may have been inherited, and for a moment I feel a romantic pull towards the image of myself pruning grapes in this ancient vineyard, with shears that have been doing the job for generations.

'How old are these vines?' I ask.

'Seven years old. We planted them when we moved here,' Mauro replies, his face full of pride as he looks across the neat rows leading all the way down to the road.

'You've only been here seven years?' I say, turning to scan my surrounds and noting the expanse of vines, the new house, the beautifully restored barn. They would have moved here about the same time we moved to the Adelaide Hills. They've been busy. 'What were you doing before that?'

'We both worked in IT. That's where we met.' Mauro lets out a small laugh. 'I don't miss it, but it made all this possible. This is a much better way to live.'

When I snip my first bunch it remains hanging from bruised, fibrous threads. There's no bite left in my elderly shears – they're gummy and good for nothing more than grabbing hold of a stalk to snap it back and deliver its weight to an open, sun-baked grave.

The boys have joined us for our first day on the job, but the heat isn't conducive to play, and there are clearly not enough pruning scissors to include them in the work. Aidan disappears after only ten minutes. 'I think I'll find Luca,' he says. But Riley hasn't settled in yet and is reluctant to leave my side. While I make my slow way along the row, he crawls into its shade. Grapes at every stage of ripeness, from green to deep purple, become his crowning glory, and Riley becomes Bacchus, the young god of wine.

This is undulating country, famous for its reds, and the hills around me are patched with squares and rectangles and odd shapes filled with grapes just weeks away from full colour. But it's even more famous for something else, and in the wide valley between this hill and the one opposite are swathes of hazelnut trees.

Bacchus emerges from his fruit bowl complaining of boredom.

'Want to know something interesting?' I say.

'Yeah. What?'

'See all those trees across the road and covering the hills?'

'Yeah.'

'They're hazelnut trees.'

'That's not very interesting.'

'No, but in a few weeks the nuts will fall from all those trees, they'll be collected and ground, and then they'll be mixed with chocolate to make Nutella.'

'Really? Is this where Nutella comes from?'

'It was invented here about two hundred years ago,' I say. 'Napoleon's doing, really. He wouldn't let the locals have as much chocolate as they liked, so they started mixing it with hazelnuts to make it go further.'

'Can we buy some and take it home?'

'I don't see why not,' I say, though really, I can see a lot of reasons why not, but it's too hot to explain them all.

'I'm going to tell Aidan,' he says, scampering out from beneath his vine. I cross my fingers that Aidan has made friends with Luca and that Riley will be welcomed into a band of three. They're starting from scratch, again, and are still in mourning for the loss of their friends at *Il Granello*. If I could speed up the process of friendship, or have any influence at all on its development, I would. But I can't do much more than cross my fingers and hope they have something in common.

Hours pass and a bell begins to sound. Before the eleventh chime, Cherie, Paul and Nicky emerge from their rows to retreat from the risen sun. I take my cue and make a mental note of which row I'm in and how far down I've come. Not far, I realise. But it also strikes me that this doesn't really matter; the frustration I might have felt at the start of this journey about a lack of progress, is absent. There's no hurry, the grapes will ripen, they'll be sweeter for my efforts, and the wine will be drunk no matter what. If it's drunk in company then any flaws will be irrelevant. I go in search of Shannon.

When I find him he's examining his vine and calculating which grapes will live to be drunk and which will die.

'Time to knock off,' I say.

'I might just finish this row,' he says, as I knew he would. I calculate he'll be another twenty minutes, so I pull the useless shears from my back pocket. This is what I'm good at, what I enjoy: noticing that Shannon needs a hand and offering it. But now that I think about it, I usually manage to time my generosity just before the task is done. He's always appreciative, but employs me in a way that drains neither time nor energy. I wonder now if he's always recognised how fragile my enthusiasm is, and is doing his best to safeguard it.

'Why don't we work the same row tomorrow?' I say. 'This is nice.'

'You'll just gasbag the whole time,' he says, grinning at me from under his hat.

'Not the whole time.'

'Then it's a date.'

We're at the end of the row when the church bells ring out a second time. Shannon's satisfied and pockets his scissors.

Back in our apartment, the boys are nowhere to be seen. We assume the best, lock the door, remove all our clothes and turn on the shower – just enough hot to take the shock out of the cold. We stand under the fall of water, uncomfortable in each other's heat, but greedy for some time alone. We stay until the steam stops rising from our skin.

'What do we do now?' I wonder out loud once we've both dressed.

'I know what you mean,' says Shannon. 'It sounds like we're going to be spoilt with time at this farm.'

'I have a feeling we're going to be spoilt with more than time,'

I say. Pia and Mauro exude generosity. After delivering us to our room and listening, in mild horror, to our affectionate account of the woodhouse at *Il Mulino* (brought on by an overwhelming sense of gratitude for a functioning ensuite bathroom), Pia sat me down and asked what we hoped to get from our stay with them. Would we, for instance, like her to arrange any excursions to other farms – perhaps somewhere that makes cheese? Were we interested in learning how to make bread, or maybe pasta? What days would we like to have off? And were we comfortable with the hours she and Mauro had arranged? We haven't been asked any of these questions before. We've been welcomed and cared for within the means of each farm, but we've always known that the main reason we're there is because our labour will make a significant contribution to productivity, and that without us, or others like us, our hosts wouldn't be able to make their lives pay. There's an ease here that's unfamiliar, but very enticing. I resolve to look for its source.

'Let's see what the boys want to do,' I say to Shannon.

Aidan, Riley and Luca sit side-by-side on an old couch on the back deck of the house. It seems they've got something in common after all. When we pull open the glass door, they completely ignore us. When we say their names, it's as if they're deaf. When Shannon ruffles Aidan's hair to alert him to our presence, he elicits a sound that could easily have been directed at an annoying fly. So far unsuccessful, Shannon places his hand in front of the small screen that has bewitched our son. The disturbance seems to register with all three, as if they're connected through some kind of gaming telepathy and a threat to one might mean a threat to all. They look up simultaneously.

'Oh. Hi, Dad, I didn't know you were there,' says Aidan. The truth of his statement is disconcerting.

'*Buongiorno*,' Luca says, before returning to his game.

Only Riley is prepared to pause. 'I'm hungry,' he says. 'Will we be having lunch soon?'

'Excellent question, sweetheart.' At times like this I'm quick to praise even the most banal conversation. 'Why don't we go and find out?'

Just as Riley's packing up his DS, Pia comes into the kitchen and sees Luca through the glass. I recognise the abrupt change in her demeanour – from easy to hard, relaxed to stressed, congenial to confrontational. Luca, sensing an increase in atmospheric pressure, shifts his weight on the couch. His right thumb keeps moving between A and B, and X and Y. His left thumb never stops applying pressure up and down, and left and right. But every now and then his eyes leave the screen to assess the situation. His mother is approaching, but it's clear that he's in the middle of a Pokémon battle, unable to save. Like children the world over, he's prepared to risk the devastation of a parental storm for the chance to evolve or level up or whatever it is that happens when you press those buttons for long enough.

Having only ever seen this interaction from the eye of the storm, I'm fascinated to watch it unfold in another family. It would be polite to leave, but I can't. I can't even begin the sequence of disengaging Aidan from his device. I think I want him to see that his mother isn't the only woman capable of going from docile to demented in under ten seconds when in competition with a screen.

Pia stands over Luca now, words spilling from her that are identical in tone to words that have spilled from me so often. Just like Aidan, Luca responds with negotiation rather than aggression, his thumbs never slowing, his eyes flicking up and down between the screen and his mum.

I register a slight increase in Pia's volume, a precursor to real trouble. Then suddenly, Luca is done. He smiles – a sure sign he managed to evolve and save – and closes his DS. Pia knows that this was a photo finish, that the winner isn't clear, and the race will be run again and again. I can see it in the deep breath she takes and the slump of her shoulders when she exhales. Then she notices me and sees a fellow sufferer. We both turn our gaze on Aidan, who is still, outrageously, absorbed in his other world. But I only have to say his name in that way that summarises a thousand previous warnings, and he closes the lid, not at all confident he can take on two irate mothers, no matter how unreasonable their demands might be.

Lunch, it turns out, will be in half an hour. I'm welcome to help, Pia says, but not obliged. She makes a blue cheese sauce, and I put water on for pasta. Luca is sent to the restaurant kitchen for bread, and I ask the boys to lay the table. Pia and I talk. It's the conversation of easy friendship, and I'm glad we've come to it so quickly. When there's a pause, I turn to check on the boys – the table is laid, and they've disappeared. Shannon is nowhere to be seen either, and I realise that he must have slipped out before the storm. Pia and I are alone, which is perfect, because I have a favour to ask.

'Pia, do you know where I could get my legs waxed?'

After four months I find myself in a state of disrepair that can only be fixed by a seasoned professional. It's been a growing concern but I've been too sheepish to voice it at other farms, worried that my vanity might not be so well-received by the hardy, unadulterated women who've fed and sheltered us. Whenever I've attempted to secure the services of an *estetista* without their help, I've been thwarted by my inadequate Italian and our lack of transport. And so, as the weeks and months have passed by, the hairs on my legs have grown strong and abundant, like weeds.

Then I saw Pia. With her smooth skin and bright-pink fingernails, she bore all the hallmarks of a maintained woman. I knew my hirsute days would soon be over and every single one of my hairs stood on end – I must have looked like a hedgehog.

Of course Pia knows where I can get my legs waxed. She reaches for her telephone book and traces her finger over various numbers. Then she looks at me, really looks at me, from head to toe.

'I could introduce you to my hairdresser too, if you like,' she says.

'I don't think our gelato budget can cover a haircut as well as a wax.'

'Okay,' she says, laughing. 'I will call the beautician for you. And if you ever want to use my hair dryer, you are very welcome.'

~

I'm on a bus to the nearby village of Bubbio for a little weeding and pruning of my own.

Bubbio is only ten kilometres away, but the road bends this way and that, and the bus stops to let people on and off, accelerating jerkily and stopping without grace. It's the first time I've been on an excursion without the family, and despite a growing queasiness in my stomach, I'm in no hurry for it to end.

Actually, I'm in no hurry for any of it to end – I love this unfettered, itinerant existence, and the challenge of trying on other people's lives – but soon we'll be home and on our own. I think Shannon is ready. I've been watching him grow into himself more and more at every farm we've stayed at; I think he's found what we came looking for and can't wait to take it back to the Adelaide Hills. Not long ago, this scared the hell out of me. I've been digging up doubts as fast as I've been digging up weeds, and remembering the joy on Shannon's face as he stuck that pitchfork into his pile of compost at *Il Granello* almost broke my heart. But now, after watching Pia and Mauro, I think it just might be possible. After all, here I am, on my way to a beautician, a few hours of pruning under my belt and the tiniest hint of a hangover reminding me of a late night and good conversation – the good life doesn't have to be exhausting and all-consuming.

We sat around the kitchen table last night drinking limoncello and grappa, while all four boys watched *The Sorcerer's Apprentice*, dubbed into Italian with English subtitles. Actually, it's an exaggeration to say we drank grappa – we really only tasted it, several times, just to confirm that it was undrinkable. We had already willingly drunk more than a few glasses of limoncello, which, it turns out, is a remarkably pleasant tipple if an Italian nonna is in charge of its production. Grappa, unfortunately, seems to be revolting no matter who's in charge of making it, but we had to be sure, and so Mauro kept pouring it into our glasses. By the time *The Sorcerer's Apprentice* had finished and the boys went to bed, we grown-ups had bonded in the age-old way.

The bus goes around another bend and I'm wondering if my breakfast will make an embarrassing appearance when I see the sign for Bubbio. I walk to the front of the bus, the doors open and I'm spat out onto the pavement. There's a small park, a bench under a large, shady tree, something resembling a breeze. I have fifteen minutes before my appointment, and everything I need to compose myself is at hand. I sit on the bench and take out my notebook to record my new enthusiasm.

By the time I enter the salon I'm perfectly well, and my sense of wellbeing increases when I inhale the concoction of scents that are characteristic of such places. It's sweet and familiar. Already I feel more beautiful.

'*Buonasera,*' I say. '*Come stai?*' I've remembered to use the appropriate afternoon greeting, and my accent is spot-on. But once again I've misled a local into believing I can understand them. The woman behind the desk prattles, probably asks my name, confirms that I'm here for a wax, enquires about just how much hair I want removed from my bikini area. I realise the inherent danger of miscommunication in this context and say, '*Non capisco l'italiano*,' employing a broad Australian drawl. Funny, suddenly I don't feel so beautiful.

'*Non capisco l'inglese*,' she replies, and her prattling stops. She leads me into a cubicle, dimly lit with all the requisite paraphernalia: a massage table covered in a towel; an assortment of tweezers, heads down in a glass of ethanol; two small electric tubs with melted wax, pink and aromatic; and beside them a pile of cloth strips and a box of tongue depressors. She points to a chair and mimes the removal of my skirt. Then she leaves.

I know the drill. I hang my skirt over the back of the chair, place my shoes under it, climb up onto the table and throw a spare towel over my furry legs. I notice that the music being piped into the room is English pop.

I sit with my arms wrapped around my knees wondering if I've been forgotten. This too is part of the drill. It takes thirty seconds to remove a skirt or jeans, and even in winter, when boots and stockings extend the undressing, it rarely takes more than a minute. But I'm always left to wait, half-naked, for interminable minutes, wondering if I've been forgotten or if another woman, in another cubicle, has just had an entire eyebrow waxed off by accident, requiring all staff to abandon their posts and try sticking on individual eyebrow hairs with that special glue they use for false eyelashes.

The door opens and a new face appears. Her smile is enormous, and so is her hair. I like her immediately, which is great, because she's about to ask me to remove the towel and spread my legs. When she speaks it's in Italian, and we re-enact my earlier conversation with her colleague. She definitely asks me to do something, but I'm not sure what. I hesitate, not wanting to respond to a simple request for my name with the full exposure of my unkempt groin. We smile a lot, giggle even, and eventually the time seems right for the removal of the towel. She leans in, as if examining my inner thighs for skin cancers. I have so much admiration for these women.

Then a serious question, one that needs an answer before she continues. I can tell by the way she looks at my crotch and flourishes her hand in the space above it, like a game show host revealing 'A brand new car!' Not a sports car, obviously, more like a people mover. The flourish is tracing a wide, circular path – it's sign language for 'How much?'

Even when conducted in English, this is a difficult conversation. There are regional variations, colloquialisms and euphemisms. The exact dimensions of a double X, for instance, can differ from salon to salon. From one, I've left feeling skinned. From another, cheated, barely able to tell the difference between the before and after shot.

A pantomime of gestures and made-up words ensues. I'm encouraged when she recognises *Brasilliano* as a legitimate word, and hope that she's heard the emphatic '*no*' that precedes it. Just in case, I direct her gaze back to the undergrowth and trace the line I want her to take. She double checks, indicates I'm being a bit conservative and runs her finger a little closer to the mid-line, I blush, nod and lie back, not at all sure what will be left when this is all over.

When I board the bus back to the farm I feel positively

aerodynamic. But I'm a bit disappointed I was so well understood. I don't think I could ever actually ask for a Brazilian or a triple X or whatever else the removal of every pubic hair might be called – mutton undressed like lamb is a phrase that springs to mind in my particular case. But the possibility of it happening by accident, and the thought of Shannon discombobulating on the discovery, became more and more appealing with every patch of hair that was ripped from my body. Another unlikely dream – they are everywhere once you start to look.

When I get back to our apartment, Shannon is snoozing. I'm hot and sticky after the walk from the bus stop so I quietly undress for a shower. Not quietly enough.

'I think she missed a patch,' Shannon says.

'What?!' I can't twist my body enough to see the back of my leg.

'Just there, it looks like a landing strip, one of those grassy ones on a remote island.' He's hardly discombobulating, but at least he's amused.

'Pass me the tweezers,' I say

'What are you going to do?'

'Pluck them all out. I'm not leaving this room until I'm as smooth as marble.'

~

The bells have been rung eight times, and are now on their second coming. We pruned the last vines days ago and have been allowed to sleep in ever since.

'I could get used to this,' I say, stretching and throwing a leg across Shannon.

'Smooth,' he says.

'Glad you noticed, it cost at least sixteen gelatos.'

'Better not tell Aidan.'

'Definitely not.'

'What could you get used to?' Shannon asks.

'This life. I reckon they've nailed it, don't you?

'It's pretty comfortable,' says Shannon.

'But still productive. They seem to have hit a sweet spot.'

'Five WWOOFers probably helps, though at the moment I think they might be struggling to keep us all busy,' he says.

On the first day after the vines, instead of handing out pruning scissors, Pia handed out spoons.

'Today, we remove weeds from the vegetable garden,' she'd said, brandishing tablespoons, dessert spoons and a couple of tarnished teaspoons. We all stood there waiting for more information.

'Maybe we'll have to eat them after we pull them out,' Shannon whispered to Riley, whose weak smile indicated he thought it might be true.

Pia noticed our confusion and continued. 'They are all you need,' she said, giving each of us a spoon relative to our size.

'Can I have a bigger one?' asked Aidan.

'If you have a bigger spoon, you have to remove bigger weeds,' Pia cautioned.

Aidan decided his teaspoon would be adequate, but I had a sudden memory of weeding around the carrot seedlings at *Pirapora*.

'Can we swap?' I asked Shannon, his tablespoon suddenly far more desirable than my dessert spoon.

'Not a chance,' he said, no doubt having a similar flashback.

It turns out Pia was right. The area given over to vegetables at *Tenuta Antica* is small – more of a patch than a commercial concern. The beds are raised and mulched, and altogether it's no bigger than the garden we have at home. So five people armed with cutlery made short work of the weeds. Before dinner, we stacked firewood.

On the second day after the vines, Pia decided that we should learn to make pasta.

'It is not possible for you to leave here without knowing how to make pasta. I would not forgive myself,' she'd said.

We spent all morning in the restaurant kitchen cracking eggs into mounds of flour and rolling the smooth, yellow dough through an electric pasta maker. Aidan donned a white hair net and apron and managed to make a sheet of pasta two metres long. It took three of us to guide it out. Like a midwife, Pia coached and encouraged, while Aidan fed the rollers and delivered the ribbon of dough into my waiting hands. His smile grew with the pasta, and when it was over, we had enough to furnish every layer of an industrial-sized lasagne. We ate the lasagne for lunch, and it fed twelve. Before dinner, we stacked firewood.

On the third day after the vines, we made bread, but not because it was required for the restaurant – Pia had that in hand. We made bread because we couldn't, and Pia didn't want anyone leaving her farm without this basic skill. All five wwooFers gathered in the kitchen where she gave us a choice of flours, counselled us on the importance of moisture and warned us not to over-knead.

As the heel of my hand pressed into the dough, I thought of Ulrike and the way she gave over her kitchen and her weekly bread, trusting, somehow, that I would work it out. Could she have known how much I craved the solitary hours of the process, even then, when time was elastic and there were no imposed schedules?

It occurred to me that Pia's kitchen couldn't have been more different than Ulrike's. Certainly, there was a similar wooden table, big enough for a crowd, but this room was well-appointed and spacious, with light streaming in from large modern windows. Nothing was cracked, and there was certainly nothing solitary about making bread in Pia's kitchen. When the instruction was over we each chose our flours, added salt and water, and mixed in our allocation of *pasta madre*. Each of us kept up a running commentary of our own progress, and it was impossible to find a rhythm in the kneading, or a quiet moment to think, for all the laughter and dire comparisons to Pia's example. When it was time to let our dough rest, we were reluctant to leave the table and good company. Coffee was made, and an hour passed quickly.

By the time our loaves were out of the oven it was clear that one of us chose too many flours, one of us didn't add enough water, and one of us over-kneaded. One of us made all three errors (it would be rude to say who) but the bread was still edible. My loaf was exactly as I'd hoped it would be, and as I inhaled its heated scent I imagined it cooling on my own kitchen bench, and the pleasure of taking the first hot slice back to where I'd laid down my notebook – one final quiet moment before the children came home from school. It was such a pleasing thought that I spread two slices with an extra thick layer of strawberry-chocolate jam, still warm from the pot, and gave them to the boys.

'This is the best bread ever,' said Aidan, clearly happy with my choice of white flour. 'Will you make it when we get home?'

'Sure,' I said.

'Do you promise?'

'I promise. Monday will be baking day, and maybe Thursday.' The thought of two baking days every week made me feel a bit giddy, and I had to sit down.

Before dinner, we stacked firewood.

On the fourth day we picked *sambuca*. It's the most minor ingredient in the aniseed drink that I was partial to knocking back during the late '80s, and in English it's known as elderberry. It felt a little more like work, especially as the sun rose and the berries became harder and harder to reach. We formed a line of production. One of us, high on a ladder, would snip bunches of ripe fruit from the tree and pass it back to another, who'd place it in a crate that would be carried to the large table in the shaded courtyard. The highest fruit were left for the birds.

'Shannon, maybe you could help me with something,' Mauro suggested after all the berries had been collected.

I was reminded how easily friendship has come to Shannon on this journey, how valued he's been for his quiet and considered

254

character, his knowledge, and his deep regard for the lives that have been shared with us. Shannon is shy, and often so short of words at social gatherings that his presence becomes peripheral. But since we've been in Italy I've noticed a flourishing. This life and the people it attracts suit him so well.

I watched as they walked in the direction of the vines, heads turned slightly towards one another, hands gesticulating, then I turned to the table where the others had begun picking the tiny black berries from their tiny crimson stalks.

The boys tried to help, for a while anyway, but they preferred plunging their hands into the bowls full of fruit – the berries like small ball bearings. Pia and I still sat together long after Cherie, Paul and Nicky had retired for the afternoon. We barely noticed the movement of our fingers for the movement of our tongues. Our boys hung around, eager to hear the stories in which they starred – their births, their schooling, their dreams (or at least the dreams we have for them – how easily I've construed Aidan's love of Lego as an ambition to be an architect). They took turns to sit on our laps or lean against us, arms around our necks. Aidan, Riley and Luca kept to their own mothers, but Daniele slid off Pia's lap to climb onto mine. When he reached his arms around my waist and rested his head against my chest it was the only time my hands stopped what they were doing. I accepted his gift with a hug of my own then I kissed his head like I'd seen Pia do on our first morning. I held his weight until every last berry had been picked from its stalk.

As the heat left the day, we stacked firewood.

~

Today we will work again. Mauro has ordered peaches from a local farmer, and we've been asked to gather in the courtyard after breakfast.

A tower of crates, full of fruit, stands beside a huge pot of water simmering on top of a gas ring. A long trestle table is set up with all manner of bowls and cutting boards and paring knives. There are two crates of peaches already dunked – their skins loosened – in the centre of the table. A bucket has been placed beside each chair. We take our seats, and Mauro shows us what's to be done.

'We will make peach juice,' he informs us, 'so all the fruit must have the skin removed and the seed taken out.' He makes quick work of the first peach, and drops its slices into one of the waiting bowls.

Hands, some still stained from *sambuca* berries, reach into the crates to retrieve their first peaches. It's a stickier job than yesterday – the fruit is ripe and juice runs down our arms and drips off the edges of the table. All four boys play table soccer nearby, stopping every now and then to pilfer segments of fruit, not interested in helping.

We each have our own process and rhythm, and soon the first bowls are full. Mauro takes them to the restaurant kitchen and empties them into an old wooden press. For the first hour it's a convivial hive of activity. We talk about our travels and other farms, about the jobs we left behind and the ones we hope to do when we return. We all agree that this is the way we should live, that working together to produce peach juice is surely the attainment of good-life nirvana.

In the second hour, those who spurned latex gloves at the start are feeling the sting of acid in tiny cuts. Backs start to ache and fingers to stiffen. The bowls we fill are constantly returned, the empty crates are removed and replaced. The peaches keep coming like a biblical plague. As each hour passes we eat fewer peaches, speak less, go to the toilet more often. Cherie asks how many crates are left, and Mauro says twenty-five. After four hours, she and Paul leave the table. The church bells are ringing, and it's time for us WWOOFers to clock off. But Shannon and I stay – Mauro and Pia will never get through it all if we don't. We work through the afternoon, and nirvana gives way to something a bit more realistic, but nonetheless satisfying.

I take a peach from the crate, slip it out of its skin and slit it down the middle. I twist and pull the two halves apart, one holds tighter to the seed than the other. My nail reaches under and levers it out, straight into the bucket on my right. I cut each half in half again, then slice it into a bowl. It took a while to settle on this procedure, but I've been doing it for six hours now and it feels automatic. I reach for another peach, but the crate is empty.

We look at each other – it's like we've come to the end of a marathon: we're exhausted but elated.

'Now to finish the juice, if you have the energy?' Mauro says.

We follow him into the kitchen where Pia is filling an old-fashioned fruit press with the last of our sliced peaches. When all the peaches are in, Mauro fits two semicircles of thick wood around a central pole, and pushes it down. The barrel that holds the fruit begins to bleed. Pulp and juice leak from the gaps and a moat around its base fills to overflowing – the dark orange nectar drips into a waiting tub. More weight is needed to extract all the juice, and Mauro piles on dense lengths of timber, then heavy cast-iron weights, the last of which has a thread to match that of the central pole. He attaches a long bar and, like a work horse, pushes it around the barrel. The pressing begins.

The kitchen fills with boys – their keen hearing must have picked up the squelch of peach pulp. We hand out glasses and let them catch the juice before it reaches the tub.

'Depending on how it tastes, we might add sugar,' says Mauro. But the consensus is that it tastes good. How could it not?

When the last drops have been extracted, the juice is bottled then put in a special oven to be pasteurised.

'My tummy hurts,' says Riley.

'I thought it might,' I say.

'Why didn't you stop me?'

'I thought it would be too cruel.'

There's no time to stack firewood this evening, and no need. We finished that job last night, and now Pia and Mauro have enough wood to fire their heaters all through the cold of winter. I wonder if they'll recall us when the pile dwindles and the chill leaves the air. It feels like we've become the best of friends, but maybe it feels like that for everyone who comes here.

~

The family is leaving tomorrow to visit a friend in Switzerland, and we WWOOFers will all go our separate ways. The table in the courtyard is set for a feast.

Mauro has made the first course and begins filling our plates with *pasta roma*. It looks like a simple tomato sauce, but tastes like so much more. 'It is my specialty,' he says.

Riley asks if he can have another serve and Mauro fills his plate. The satisfaction of pleasing a fussy eater is written all over his face.

The pasta is followed by Nonna's roasted veal, which is followed by a crisp salad picked by the boys and me this afternoon. It's only when we get to dessert that there's a departure from the Italian habit of honouring good food and produce through separate courses. Trifle is Cherie's farewell gift. It took all afternoon to construct, and when it came to the table it was a work of art, each layer of strawberries and kiwifruit so precise that it was a shame to disturb it. But disturb it we did, and now we ache with regret.

Night has fallen over the courtyard, and only the children have the energy to move. They're hunting frogs, following their evening call and disturbing them in their watery hideouts. The rest of us are stuffed and stuck at the table.

'How long have you known her?' I ask Pia, of the woman they'll visit in Switzerland.

'She came here as a WWOOFer, years ago, soon after we

started this life, and we became friends, like you and me.' She touches my forearm, which is resting on the table beside hers. 'Daniele loves her. When she came, he clung to her like she was his mother. Switzerland is not that far, so we try to visit with each other every year or so.'

'Do you think you'd ever visit Australia?' I ask. I've asked it of others, but I knew it was not a real possibility. It's too far and too expensive for near-subsistence farmers to even contemplate. But Pia and Mauro are not subsistence farmers, they've built this life on savings from good jobs, and I have a feeling they don't need to rely completely on income from the farm.

'Yes, of course. We're thinking of coming in the next few years. Actually, having you here has made us think it is possible to travel with the boys, maybe to be WWOOFers in Australia. But we have to wait for Daniele to grow up a bit. He would not make us welcome at the moment.'

This is our last night in Italy, and I feel like something is slipping through my fingers. I want to hang on to it but I'm not sure how.

'We'd welcome you,' I say. 'Maybe you could be our first WWOOFers?' It's a genuine offer, but even as I say it I don't expect it to happen.

The Adelaide Hills

(Bake bread)

———

I can't sleep. We've been home for three days and still I can't sleep.

'It's just jet lag,' Shannon says. 'Try thinking of something monotonous and boring.'

'All I can think about is Ulrike's *pasta madre*. I think I've done something really stupid.'

When the *pasta madre* had dried in the hot Tuscan sun it looked like a cake of heroin. At least I think it did. I actually don't know what a cake of heroin looks like, but we joked about it at the time. I put it in the pocket at the back of my pack and pretty much forgot about it. Until we arrived at the train station on our way to the airport. There was an announcement about what to do if you saw a suspicious package, and from that moment my foil-wrapped bread starter began a process of mental fermentation that had me in such an agitated state I would have ticked all the boxes for a strip search.

'What have you done?' Shannon asks sleepily.

'I posted it.'

'The *pasta madre*?'

'Yes.'

'Where? When?'

'At the station, on our way to the airport.'

'Why did you post it?'

'I thought we'd get in trouble if I brought it into Australia.'

'You should've just binned it.'

'I know that now, but I wasn't thinking straight.'

I didn't want to leave Italy. I'd settled into our nomadic life, and moving slowly had become second nature. As we packed for the last time I came across my foil-wrapped memory of Tuscany and was overwhelmed. I thought about throwing it away ten times between *Tenuta Antica* and the train station, but at the last minute I let an image of Ulrike's bread filling my kitchen with its familiar aroma guide my hand. I bought stamps and an envelope, wrote my name and address in clear block letters, slipped in the *pasta madre*, licked the flap and sealed it. Then I dropped the package in a letter box.

'I wouldn't worry. It will either turn up, or it won't. Now try and sleep.'

But I can't. By the time Shannon's breathing has slowed I've let the night take hold, and it's easy to imagine the discovery of my foil package and the massive police operation it will initiate. I see the farm in Tuscany being raided by Interpol, Ulrike dragged from her kitchen and the dough on her hands scraped off and bagged as evidence. When the wind blows against the side of our house, I imagine it's the federal police breaking down the door to search for other contraband. I pull the covers up tight around my neck and wonder what the penalty is for bringing seed and grain into Australia without declaring it.

When I finally sleep, I find myself in a small room. A desk lamp the only illumination, its light blinding. I endure hours of questioning about what I intend to do with the package, and though I try, I can't remember exactly how to make a sourdough loaf. As the sun rises on my nightmare, I finally cave in and admit that my real plan was to crush the contents into a fine powder and sell it on the street for $200 a hit.

In the morning, Shannon suggests I call customs and fess up. Customs put me onto quarantine, who put me onto a lovely man called Paul, who explains that my starter was likely to be destroyed, but if it did arrive in the post I could pop in and have it examined as a courtesy to the Australian public.

~

The *pasta madre* hasn't arrived. After four weeks I expect it won't, and I'm deeply disappointed. I wouldn't have a clue how to make it from scratch, and this is reason enough to buy a loaf at Woolworths, even though I have all the time in the world and a financial imperative to make my own.

I'm tired. I have a feeling that I brought something valuable back from Italy, but I can't remember what it is. I look at photos to jog my memory, but the longer I stare at them the more Italy seems to be turning into a still life. When I look out at the carpet of soursob that has grown out of control during the wet Hills winter, I have an uneasy sense of having been nowhere at all.

Raspberries. They fill the photo I've landed on, and I remember thinking I'd never seen so many, and how spoilt we were to be eating them by the fistful when they were $6.99 a punnet at the supermarket back home. The boys grazed like the offspring of gods that day. Stefan showed them how they could push a blackcurrant inside the cavity of a raspberry and create a taste sensation that rivalled any they'd find in the confectionary aisle. Their fingers and faces were stained with the pleasure of it. But I'm torn between this image and the memory of Elisa weeping. As worthy as it is, I just can't imagine myself as a farmer, and I know now that it will barely pay its way.

So I sit here, contemplating the soaking rain and the fertile land it falls on, wondering how to tell Shannon that going to Italy has been like trying on a dress that looks fabulous on the mannequin and realising that, as much as I want it to, it just doesn't fit.

He wraps my hand around a glass. It's hot, half-filled with coffee, just as Romano would make it.

'I need to get a job,' I say to him.

'Yeah, you do, we're broke. It'll be a while before this farm earns its keep.'

'I need it for more than money.' I can't look him in the eye, so I keep looking out the window.

He sits beside me, looking out at the garden.

'I don't think I want it anymore,' I say.

'What do you mean?'

'I thought I loved it before we left. But now I think I just loved the idea of it. I don't think I can do what Stefan and Ulrike do. I don't think I want to work that hard; there'd be no time for anything else, and no money.'

'I know what you mean.' He puts his arm around my shoulders. 'The thought of removing all that soursob makes my stomach turn. I barely know where to start, and right now it's hard to imagine this will ever be a going concern.'

'But you wouldn't want to give it up, would you?'

'Of course not.' He holds me tighter, as if he thinks I might fall. 'I think we should give ourselves some time to settle back in. See how we feel about everything once we get back into some sort of routine.

'But if I get a job, we're back where we started.'

'No, we're not. We hadn't been to Italy when we started,' he says.

'I flip-flop between wishing we'd never gone and desperately wanting to be back there.'

'Why do you wish we'd never gone?'

'Because then I could still be dreaming.'

He's silent for a long time.

'Do you remember when we were stacking wood at Pia and Mauro's?' he says.

'Which time? We stacked wood a lot at Pia and Mauro's.'

'Towards the end. We had a production line going because the pile had reached the roof of the shed. You were at the bottom, I was at the top and everyone else was in between.'

'Oh, yeah. It was quite a celebration when I picked up that last piece of wood.'

'It was. And afterwards we sat in the dirt looking up at this monument we'd built and you said you might write about it.'

'About the wood stack?'

'Not the wood stack, about our Italian summer. About weeding our way around Italy.'

'Did I?'

'You know you did.'

I can feel my heart rate quicken. 'That would be quite an undertaking.'

'It might help.'

'It wouldn't help you. Writing a book takes time. You'd be stuck in the garden all by yourself.'

'Pip, that's exactly where I want to be. As long as you're nearby, doing something you want to be doing, I'll be happy.'

~

A loaf of Ulrike's rye is cooling on the kitchen table when Shannon comes in from the garden. The hint of coriander is unmistakable.

'It's about time,' he says, pulling off his boots.

'Well, I had to make my own *pasta madre*, it takes a while.'

'Not six months.'

'No, not six months.'

'So what's changed?'

'I've been writing about *Il Mulino*. Do remember Ulrike's salad bowl?'

'No. Why should I remember her salad bowl?'

'No reason. It was a cheap plastic bowl with a crack in the bottom.'

'So what's so special about it?'

'It was good enough, even though it leaked.'

He looks at me, puzzled, but decides to cut a slice of bread instead of quizzing me further. Steam rises and we're back there, in Ulrike's kitchen.

Postscript
(A good enough life)

From my desk, I can see Shannon in the veggie patch. He's tidying up before our first WWOOFers arrive. He wants to make a good impression, and I can't help thinking of Elisa cleaning all the floors and windows of her three-storey farmhouse in preparation for her first WWOOFers.

I'm doing what I've been doing ever since Shannon suggested I write it all down, over a year ago. I've discovered more of Italy and understood more of myself through this second journey of words. I've come to realise that dreams, when dormant, are nothing more than pretty postcards for places we want to go, people we want to be. Travelling with a dream is another thing altogether. Like the twister in *The Wizard of Oz*, my dream has picked me up, shaken me about and put me back where I started. Nothing looks quite the same; so much that was dull is brighter.

It took time to dismantle the framework of the life we thought we were building. When we did, we realised there was a lot to be salvaged, that more than one way of life could be accommodated on the foundations we'd laid. Shannon was back into the garden within a month, and as the orchard began to blossom his mood lifted. I never got back into the garden, at least not in the way I thought I would before going to Italy. I'm not short on ideas, and I can be relied on for weeding every long weekend, but my perspective has changed and so have my dreams. We spent some dark months working out how these new dreams could cohabit with the old.

A job helped, eventually. At first I thought it was a defeat, but I think I'd have gone mad without it. I enjoy the company of the strangers who catch my bus, and the buzz of ideas that reverberate through the hive of my office block. And sometimes, during my lunch break, I sit at Lucia's in the Adelaide Central Market and pretend I'm in Lucca, watching people going about their day. We'd struggle if it wasn't for my income, but this time around, my job isn't the dominant colour in the landscape of our lives. It isn't my job that dictates my mood or how much wine I drink or how much energy I have for making raspberry jam with the boys. It's part-time and contained, so I have whole days when the house is empty and there is nothing to do but make bread and fill the idle hours between kneading and baking with words.

I'm beginning to understand the legacy of our time in Italy. To an observer, our life would look almost exactly the same as it was before we went searching for something more. But there's one significant difference: life is good. Not because we're living the dream – that will always be elusive, it's the nature of dreams. But in searching for ours, we've found something else.

We've found an appreciation for things that are a privilege and that have been there all along, and we've found the courage to explore our deepest selves.

Our life is good because it's good enough. All it ever required was a bit of tweaking, a measure of honesty, and one or two small compromises. But we needed to dwell a while in others' lives to understand that. Every family we stayed with had built the life they shared with us on a dream not so different to ours. For most it was a little tarnished, the reality not quite what they had in mind. But for all of them there was meaning and real value in the time and energy they spent working on the land that fed them. For Lauren, like me, it might not have been enough. Soon after our stay, she and Gianni left *Pirapora* and moved to the UK. The last I heard, they were WWOOFing their way around the world.

Italy has shown us who we are, and we're grateful. We're particularly grateful to Stefan, who taught us to stay calm and never interrupt a meal to fix something. And Ulrike, who taught me to move slowly and need less. And Romano and Elisa, who taught us that coffee is best served in a glass, and that whistling 'Don't Worry, Be Happy' can cure backache and heartache, especially if others join in. And Pia, who proved dirt and pink fingernails can be happy bedfellows. And Mauro, whose love of wine and a healthy financial plan helped build a dream that looks a little bit like the brochures. And Gianni, who never failed to put good food on the table. And Lauren, who showed me myself and challenged my dreaming – I didn't fully understand it then, and I failed to be grateful.

And there are others to thank: the street vendors, the violin player, and the ghosts who walked up and down the aisles of trains from Rome to Zambrone, Matera to Turin. A good enough life is a privilege.

Tomorrow will be Christmas day, and at five in the morning our first WWOOFers will arrive on a bus from Victoria. When Aidan and Riley look under the Christmas tree, among the gifts will be four Italians, already unwrapped and ready to play. The boys will not be shy because they'll know them – Pia and Mauro, Luca and Daniele – they're coming, after all.

'For us to go to Italy and to penetrate into Italy is like a most fascinating act of self-discovery.'

DH Lawrence, Sea and Sardinia

Acknowledgements

This book exists because of the support, encouragement and expertise of so many.

Heartfelt thanks to my editor, Ruby Ashby-Orr, for understanding what was important right from the start, and for being so generous, courteous and clear throughout. And thanks to the whole team at Affirm Press – Martin Hughes, Keiran Rogers, Grace Breen, Kate Goldsworthy, Stephanie Bishop-Hall, Rosslyn Almond and Christa Moffitt – for everything they have done to turn my words into a book.

I am deeply grateful to Carol Lefevre for showing me how to 'turn a sentence', and for the Arts South Australia 'Independent Makers and Presenters Grant' that allowed me to work with her during the drafting of this book. I am also grateful to Sarah Tooth from the South Australian Writers Centre and the community of students and teachers who have taught me something about observing and writing about life.

I would like to thank the following people for reading early drafts and providing much needed encouragement and feedback: Suzanne Verral, Islwyn Williams, Nicola Williams, Mary McCune, Gwenda Garred, Anji Hill, Evan Jones and Richard Walsh. Special thanks also to Christine McCabe and Max Anderson for squeezing this book into their busy lives just before it went to print.

This story started as a series of emails to friends, who all encouraged me to write the book. Thanks to all my mates at the Centre for Work + Life for sending me off on this journey knowing I was unlikely to return. And love and gratitude to all of the following: Ali Elder for holding my hand when I needed a hand to hold; Andrea Tunbridge and Tim Verschoyle for providing a peaceful place to write; Jolie Thomas, Margi Sarre, Rebekah Clarkson and Suzie Riley for making life in the Adelaide Hills especially good; Vanessa Isles, Anne Beath, Lou Belle Barrett, Andrea Brydges, Krista Brydges and Jane Lawson, for staying close when we are not; and to Lisa Harrison, for putting pen to paper and encouraging other dreams to fly.

I am so grateful to my mum, Peggy Williams, for believing I can do anything even when I'm certain I can't. And to my dad, Islwyn Williams, who is a writer and a dreamer and has been the most magnificent role model in both cases.

Of course, this book would be nothing if not for the people who shared their lives with us. I hope my gratitude is woven through these pages.

And finally, to Aidan and Riley, thank you for all that you teach me, every day of your lives. And to Shannon, a dream come true – thank you for everything.